Christianity for S...

Christianity for Beginners

Tommy Cannon and Bobby Ball

Hodder & Stoughton
LONDON SYDNEY AUCKLAND

British Library Cataloguing in Publication Data
A record for this book is available from the British Library

ISBN 0 340 62146 X

Typeset by Hewer Text Composition Services, Edinburgh
Printed and bound in Great Britain by
Cox & Wyman Ltd, Reading, Berks

Hodder and Stoughton Ltd
A Division of Hodder Headline PLC
338 Euston Road
London NW1 3BH

This book is dedicated to
everyone seeking God

Acknowledgments

We would like to thank the following people for their help and consideration while we were writing this book.

TOMMY: I would like to thank my wife, Hazel, and my children, Kelly and Zoe, for their patience and understanding.

BOBBY: I would like to thank Barry Pettifer, Chris Gidney, Dave Bemment and Ray Bevan for their fellowship and love over the years. And last but certainly not least, my wife Yvonne, for understanding when I didn't lie around the swimming pool with her when we were in America!

Thank you.

Tommy Cannon and Bobby Ball.

Contents

Introduction   1

1. Is God Real?   5
2. Is the Bible True?   15
3. Who Is Jesus?   31
4. Why Come to God?   53
5. Coming to God   69
6. Growing as a Christian   83
7. Spiritual Warfare   103
Epilogue   119

Introduction

Dear friend,

We believe that becoming a Christian, or starting to get to know God, means taking a series of steps. The good news is that by reading this book, you may well have taken one of them! We need to make it clear, though, that just reading this book will not automatically make you a Christian. One of the steps is starting to think seriously about God, and we hope this book will help. We won't underestimate God!

We don't want you to think that because we have written a book about Christianity, we were always spiritual people. Oh, no! And we emphasise that! We were two of the least spiritual people you could never wish to meet.

BOBBY: (I am the small, good-looking one with the moustache.) I lived a life that was full of pain, greed, lust and selfishness. I lived life just to satisfy me. I didn't care about anybody else but myself. That's how I lived until one day a man told me something was missing from my life, and that was Jesus Christ. I thought he was crazy, but somewhere deep down inside, I knew he had spoken the truth. To cut a long story short, from that moment, I started to search for Jesus and I found him. The strange thing was that he had been waiting for me all the time. I was just too caught up in myself to realise it. From that day, he came to live with me and my life changed completely. Now I can't imagine how I ever lived without him.

TOMMY: (Ignore what Bobby says about him being good-looking, because I'm the good-looking one.) Not only that, I'm taller than him. God meets people in many different ways. In Bobby's case, he had an empty feeling inside himself for months, a feeling that something was missing from his life. But in my case, it seemed that suddenly I realised I needed Jesus, and just gave my life to him. Looking back now, I can see that God sort of romanced me. He slowly worked his way into my heart. I saw the difference in Bobby's life, and I saw Christians around me living lives that seemed fulfilled, and then almost before I knew it, *boom!* – God came into my life and totally changed it.

After we became Christians, we read many books. Some were wonderful and inspirational and spoke about Jesus with a clear and spiritual message. But there are a lot of religious books about that you need a degree in theology to understand. And not everyone has got a degree in theology! So we decided to write a book about God and about Christianity that wasn't too theological. We had to ask ourselves some tough questions before we became Christians, and our book tries to answer some of them.

The first three chapters try to sort out some problems about God, the Bible and Jesus. We believe you can trust what the Bible says about God and his Son, Jesus, but many people just dismiss it all as fairytales. Often that's because they don't know what the Bible says. Nearly all of what we want to say is based on the Bible, and we quote it a lot. We want to suggest here that you look up the passages we quote in a good modern translation of the Bible – one without too many 'thees' and 'thous'! We use the New International Version (NIV), and we put all the references in brackets. If you don't know where to find a passage in the Bible, there's a contents page after the preface and before Genesis. But remember there are several books called 'John'! In each book, all the chapters are numbered, and the verses are numbered within the chapters. So 'John 3:16' means the Gospel of John, chapter 3 and verse 16. You'll get used to it after a while, and we hope you'll enjoy looking at what the Bible really says.

The next chapters ask why we should look for God, and why we don't bother to. And then we look at what faith is. Next and most important, we talk about the steps you can take to become a Christian, and how you can live a fulfilled life with God. Being a Christian isn't always easy, but we believe God has got a great sense of humour. You don't have to be all straight and serious when you're a Christian. We've put some jokes in because that's what we're good at, and because we think God is the sort of person who likes people to be happy. He created laughter, and there's joy in heaven when people become Christians (Luke 15:7).

So read on, dear friend. We hope you enjoy the book and learn something from it that you can use in your life. Our prayers and thoughts are with you.

Chapter 1

Is God Real?

Let's start at the beginning. Nobody is going to believe in God and become a Christian unless they can first believe that God is real. Now we know he is real because we've met him, and we talk to him every day! But if you haven't met him yet, it can sound a bit strange talking as if everybody knows God is real. Our society tends to assume he isn't, or that if he is real, he is very far away and not at all interested in what we do with our lives.

You might ask, 'How can you be sure God is real?' Well, we can't prove it by a scientific experiment, but there is evidence. Changed lives prove he is real, for one thing. But think for a minute about the times when you've watched someone in distress on television, and a tear has come into your eye. Or you've seen a child crying, and you wanted to pick them up and comfort them. Or you've felt angry at the injustice suffered by someone who has been injured or robbed. It's very hard to explain why we should feel compassion or love for people we don't know and are never likely to meet, but we do. If we just happen to be here by chance, there can be no very good reason why we should be concerned about anything.

Science

Science can explain a lot of things. But scientists can only give part of the explanation for how we reason, why different emotions affect us in different ways, how our speech developed, or why systems of morality might have developed. These are things that set us apart from the animals. Now if all our emotions and intellect can be explained as chemical and electrical changes in our brains and bodies, why don't animals have them too? And if it's all to do with evolution, why didn't the animals evolve in a similar way to humans?

We're not knocking science, but we aren't satisfied that science has all the answers. Centuries ago, a Hebrew writer wrote that God created men and women in his own image. In other words, God made us different from the animals. And our emotions and reason reflect God in a special way. Sometimes we can live as if God wasn't real, and refuse to feel for other people, and concentrate only on ourselves. But as soon as we start to think about the purpose of life, God starts to come into the frame. You don't have to believe in cooking or in cooks until you eat a cooked meal! In the same way, you don't have to believe in God until you start thinking where we and the world came from, and why on earth it's here!

God Changed Me

TOMMY: Take a look at me!

BOBBY: Do we have to, Tom?

TOMMY: I'll ignore that! I lived for years in a way that not many people knew about. I lied, I cheated, I hurt people. But to the general public I played out the role of Mr Nice Guy. Sometimes I wish I had never been Tommy Cannon, with fame and wealth, because it made it easy for me to sin and ignore God. Why should I come to God? I had what I wanted, or thought I wanted. I didn't want to know about God. But once I let myself think that God is real, I found that he is, and he changed my life! Now I'm not so wealthy and famous, but I know God has forgiven me, and I'm a happier man than I ever was before. And I know that God is not just for Bobby and me, but for everyone.

You can reject God, and I'm sure that hurts him just as it hurts us when people reject us. You can pretend that you believe God is real – this way you find how easy it is to do things that show you don't really believe! Or you can accept God, and his power which gives you the help you need to live as if God's ways really matter.

I will never forget when my mother was dying. She was not far from death and in a coma, when suddenly she woke up and started to recite the Lord's Prayer. She was so ill, that it must have been something, or someone, very powerful that brought her out of the coma to make her peace with God. It certainly had a great effect on me.

I've now been a Christian for more than four years, and Bobby for ten. We've tested God in our lives and we know we're not fooling ourselves that he is real.

BOBBY: Tommy's right about that! You can't really know that God is real until you have faith and trust him. Science can't prove the existence of God, but of course it can't disprove his existence either. Scientists have changed the face of the earth with nuclear power, computers, and all kinds of technology, but they will never be able to disprove the existence of God even if they wanted to.

For me, the complexity of life forms and the ability of our brains to take in information show that God must exist. How could it all be the result of an accident, a big bang? And if it was a big bang, where did the bang come from and why did it bang? The Bible says that God created it all from nothing, which is in many ways similar to what the big bang theory says — but God *intended* it to happen as it did, and designed the complexity. The world shows God to be powerful and creative.

People think that I talked Tommy into becoming a Christian, but this is a long way from the truth. Sure, I was a Christian for six years before Tommy, but in fact we rarely talked about God. It was Tommy's own need that drew him to God, and he had to find God for himself. It's the same for all of us: we won't prove God scientifically, because you can't measure him, or weigh him, or put him in a test tube. You can only look at the evidence, find out what Christians believe and ask God to make himself known. You know he's real when you experience him for yourself. If you just say 'I don't believe', it might be because you haven't taken the trouble to find out.

God Is not a Dictator

Knowing God is not something that can be forced on you. If God forced you to believe in him, he would be a dictator, and there aren't many people who love dictators. God wants us to love him as he loves us. That kind of love can only be based on faith, because it has to be given freely. You can look at the evidence for God and find that it is very strong, but even that won't make you a Christian. You need faith to respond to God's love.

TOMMY: That's what happened to me. I had always believed in something 'out there', a powerful force, a God, whatever. I wasn't a hundred per cent sure, but I thought I'd better believe something in case when I died there was a something! Like millions of other people I was unsure and a bit scared. Like millions of other people I was getting the worst of both worlds – unsure and scared now, and uncertain about what happens when I die.

Anyway, Bobby asked me to go to church with him one Sunday morning because his daughter was having her son 'dedicated' (sort of thanking God for the baby, and asking God to look after him). I really didn't want to go. I'd rather have played golf. I agreed to go but it had been years since I last went to church and I was dreading it. I could imagine what it was going to be like – it would be cold, boring, and the place would be full of cold-faced 'Christians'. But I went. As we were working in South Wales at the time, we went to stay with a friend of Bobby's who was pastor of a church there. I wasn't looking forward to it at all when Sunday morning came round.

Bobby and I gathered with our respective families, and before I knew where I was I was in the church building and surrounded by Christians. But they didn't seem like most of the Christians I had met before. They were friendly and joyful. They were shaking my hand and hugging me and showing that they loved me. I didn't even know these people! It felt really strange, but very good! And then we had the service, which was not at all what I had expected: there was brilliant singing, which really carried you along, and the message the pastor gave was simple and true. At the end, he asked if anyone would like to commit their life to God, and something made me put my hand up. There I was in this church, that I hadn't wanted to come to, with my hand up in the air, committing myself to a God I hadn't been sure about. The pastor prayed with me, and I felt strange, somehow as if I was a different person. If you'd asked me then if I believed in God, I would have said yes, but I still wasn't absolutely sure.

It was about a week later that I became sure God is real. I had woken up, and my wife was downstairs, so I was alone. I'm not sure to this day what it was, but I got an overwhelming longing to pray. I hadn't prayed since the day I was in church. I got down on my knees at the side of the bed and opened my heart to God. I told him my innermost thoughts and feelings (as if he didn't know). I confessed all the wrong things in my life to him and asked him to forgive me. Suddenly I felt a warmth flow through me, and I got very emotional. It was at that moment I knew God was real. I felt clean, and for the first time in my life I had something to believe in other than myself. For once I wasn't trying to control God and trying to force him to answer all my questions. I was letting him open my eyes to the truth, and experiencing him as a person, not as a something! Reaching out to him in faith is what convinces you he is real.

Faith

Later on, we're going to talk about faith a bit more. But everything we do in life takes a bit of faith. When our friends and family say that they care about us, we believe them, even when they're not there. When we eat our food we believe it will be good for us and not poison. Every time we switch on a light, we have faith that the electricity is there and the light will come on. Even science, which sometimes tries to do without God, can only be carried on in faith, believing that there are explanations for the way chemicals and electrical impulses behave.

Believing in God is similar, but maybe not quite the same. You have to reach out, just as you do to switch on the light, or eat food. But God is a person, and he expects a response from us, and a relationship with us. When you switch on a light your responses are automatic: your eyes adjust to the brightness by making the pupils smaller. But with God, the response is not automatic. As with any relationship, you have to decide where it is going. God wants to change us and make us better people, but we have to give him permission. We have to ask him, even! Because as we said before, he doesn't force himself on people.

Changing Hearts

God is the only one who can change the human heart. Medicine can make us live longer, inventions can make life easier. We can travel further and faster than ever before. But for all our technology, there are more wars, there is more poverty, more famine, more hatred, misery, greed and crime now than ever before. We think we are going forward and progressing, but actually when you think about it, we're going backwards. That's because the material, physical things don't get to the heart of the matter. They don't make us rich in our souls, and sometimes they mask the emptiness we feel.

TOMMY: Bobby and I went to Wormwood Scrubs Prison to talk to the 'lifers'. After we had had coffee with them we just sat and talked. A man came up to me and said that he had been ordained as a minister of the church while he was in prison. I asked him what he was in for, and he told me he had killed his best friend. He had asked God's forgiveness, and had given his life to God. I am not condoning the murder, and he wouldn't want me to. But it shows how God can change lives whatever the circumstances, and wherever you are. Often it's people we might not expect to turn to God, who realise they most need him. In John's Gospel it says, 'To all who received him, to those who believed in his name, he gave the right to become children of God' (John 1:12). No conditions! You don't have to be the right sort of person to apply!

BOBBY: I get letters from a man in prison who murdered his two children. I can't go into details about how it happened, but of course he is torn with grief about what he has done. He was kept under constant watch in case he tried to commit suicide. He couldn't find any way of easing his mind of the guilt. Finally he turned to God, and God helped him. God doesn't condone what people have done, any more than we do, but he can deal with it. This story, and the one Tommy has just told, shows that God can change lives in a way that technology can't. God is changing millions of lives every day.

God is real, but you have to find him for yourself. Nobody else can do it for you. And he isn't going to pop up out of a book as if by magic. If you think this book will do it, you'll be disappointed. You have to think it out for yourself, think whether this world is all there is, or whether there is more truth to be discovered through faith. This world doesn't satisfy, and riches, sex, fame and power soon fade. But the love of God does satisfy, and it does have a future, and it never fades.

Chapter 2

Is the Bible True?

BOBBY: Tommy, before we discuss whether the Bible is true or not, can you answer this question?

TOMMY: I'll try, Bobby.

BOBBY: Were the epistles the wives of the apostles?

TOMMY: Your jokes are getting worse!

What is the Bible?

The Bible is not just a book about people riding around in the desert on camels, or fairy stories about Father Christmas, or tales for children. It's actually a compilation of sixty-six books written by all sorts of people: fishermen, a doctor, a

king, various scholars, people from very varied
walks of life. Some had little education, some
had a lot. Some actually walked around with
Jesus and talked and worked with him. Some
talk about miracles happening, some write po-
etry, some write laws or proverbs. Some books
are letters about how churches can grow in the
Christian faith. One book doesn't even mention
God! Some books were written about two thousand years ago, some much longer ago. But the
amazing thing about all these books is that God
speaks through them, in such a way that we can
say that 'the Bible says' this or that, because it is
so consistent in what it shows us of God.

Prophecy

All kinds of prophecies appear in the Bible. We
just want to mention a few so that you get the
general picture. You might want to look the
references up in a Bible.

The book of Genesis tells us that God made a
promise to Abraham, who lived around two
thousand years before Jesus, so nearly four
thousand years ago.

The LORD said to Abram . . . 'I will make

your offspring like the dust of the earth, so that if anyone could count the dust, then your offspring could be counted' (Gen. 13: 14–16).

'LORD' is spelled like that in the Old Testament section of the NIV Bible because the word was thought by the Jewish writers to be holy. Abram (which means something like 'the father is exalted') changed his name to Abraham (which means 'the father of many nations') later in the story, in Genesis 17:5. And later, God said,

'Look up at the heavens and count the stars – if indeed you can count them.' Then he said to him, 'So shall your offspring be' (Gen. 15:5).

Abraham had one or two problems here. He was very old, and his wife Sarah was well past childbearing age. But God did as he promised, and at the age of ninety-nine, Abraham had a son by Sarah. Today it is estimated that there are fourteen million Jewish people. Both Jewish and Arab peoples trace their descent from Abraham.

That's a prophecy that has major importance today. But what about Nahum? It's a little book, that's hard to find. Nahum lived in the seventh century before Christ. He said this about the oppressive city of Nineveh, capital of the Assyrian empire: 'He will make an end of Nineveh; he will pursue his foes into darkness' (Nahum 1:8). And again,

> The LORD has given a command concerning you, Nineveh: 'You will have no descendants to bear your name. I will destroy the carved images and cast idols that are in the temple of your gods. I will prepare your grave, for you are vile' (Nahum 1:14).

And at the end,

> O king of Assyria, your shepherds slumber; your nobles lie down to rest. Your people are scattered on the mountains with no-one to gather them. Nothing can heal your wound; your injury is fatal. Everyone who hears the news about you claps his hands at your fall, for who has not felt your endless cruelty? (Nahum 3:18–19).

When Nahum made these prophecies, Assyria was the most powerful nation on earth. It would be like saying that a hundred years from now,

New York would be destroyed, and lost without trace. But in 612 BC, Nineveh was overthrown, and the site in northern Iraq is now named Tell Kuyunjik, 'mound of many sheep' – a name which shows that the site was deserted and used for grazing.

Prophecies about Jesus

About seven hundred years before Jesus was born, a prophet called Micah said,

> You, Bethlehem Ephrathah, though you are small among the clans of Judah, out of you will come for me one who will be ruler over Israel, whose origins are from of old, from ancient times (Mic. 5:2).

At Jesus' birth, this prophecy was fulfilled:

> After Jesus was born in Bethlehem in Judea, during the time of King Herod, Magi from the east came to Jerusalem and asked, 'Where is the one who has been born king of the Jews? We saw his star in the east and have come to worship him' (Matt. 2:1–2).

When King Herod asked the leaders of the
Jewish people of the time where the Christ or
Messiah (the one specially appointed by God to
save his people) was to be born, they referred to
this prophecy (Matt. 2:5–6).

Isaiah, a prophet from about the same time as
Micah, prophesied about Jesus' trial and death.
God's special servant would be ill-treated, and he
says this: 'I offered my back to those who beat me,
my cheeks to those who pulled out my beard; I did
not hide my face from mocking and spitting' (Isa.
50:6). After Jesus' trial, Matthew tells us that
'They spat in his face and struck him with their
fists. Others slapped him . . .' (Matt. 26:67).

Isaiah again speaks of Jesus when he says that
God's servant

> was led like a lamb to the slaughter, and as a
> sheep before her shearers is silent, so he did
> not open his mouth. By oppression and
> judgment he was taken away. And who
> can speak of his descendants? For he was
> cut off from the land of the living; for the
> transgression of my people he was stricken.
> He was assigned a grave with the wicked,
> and with the rich in his death, though he had
> done no violence, nor was any deceit in his
> mouth (Isa. 53:7–9).

And again, 'He poured out his life unto death, and was numbered with the transgressors. For he bore the sin of many, and made intercession for the transgressors' (Isa. 53:12). All this came true as Jesus was tried and crucified. Jesus did not speak in his own defence at his trial; the court which tried him was rigged; he was crucified with common robbers and murderers; his grave (for a while, at least) was borrowed from the rich man, Joseph of Arimathea; and just before he died, he prayed that God would forgive those who were crucifying him. You can read this at the end of all the Gospels – Matthew, Mark, Luke and John.

Jesus' Own Understanding of Prophecy

Jesus understood some Bible passages and prophecies as referring especially to himself. At the very beginning of his ministry he taught the people in his own town, reading the words of Isaiah:

'The Spirit of the Lord is on me, because he has anointed me to preach good news to the poor. He has sent me to proclaim freedom to the prisoners and recovery of sight to the blind, to release the oppressed, to proclaim the year of the Lord's favour.'

Then he [Jesus] rolled up the scroll, gave it back to the attendant and sat down. The eyes of everyone in the synagogue were fastened on him, and he began by saying to them, 'Today this scripture is fulfilled in your hearing' (Luke 4:18–21 and Isa. 61:1–2).

When people started trying to trick Jesus by quoting the Bible at him, he said the same as we have already said: just knowing things about God isn't the same as knowing God:

You diligently study the Scriptures because you think that by them you possess eternal life. These are the Scriptures that testify about me, yet you refuse to come to me to have life (John 5:39–40).

Then, as he was dying on the cross, Jesus saw one of the most moving psalms fulfilled in his own experience. He felt utterly cut off from his Father: 'Jesus cried out in a loud voice . . . "My God, my God, why have you forsaken me?"' (Matt. 27:46 and Ps. 22:1).

Jesus' Prophecies

Not only that, but Jesus also prophesied, especially about his death, and long before it happened. As soon as Jesus' followers started to understand that he was the Messiah, he told them that he was going to be killed. Because of the amazing things Jesus did, all sorts of rumours circulated about him, and one day Jesus asked what people were saying:

'Some say [you are] John the Baptist; others say Elijah; and still others, that one of the prophets of long ago has come back to life.'

'But what about you?' he [Jesus] asked. 'Who do you say I am?'

Peter answered, 'The Christ of God.'

Jesus . . . said, 'The Son of Man [meaning himself] must suffer many things and be rejected by the elders, chief priests and teachers of the law, and he must be killed and on the third day be raised to life' (Luke 9:19–22).

There were many other occasions on which Jesus predicted his death and his resurrection.

Jesus not only predicted these things about

himself, he also made prophecies about the world. He knew that the world would come to an end, and that in the last days of the world there would be terrible things happening.

> Watch out that no-one deceives you. For many will come in my name, claiming, 'I am the Christ,' and will deceive many. You will hear of wars and rumours of wars, but see to it that you are not alarmed. Such things must happen, but the end is still to come. Nation will rise against nation, and kingdom against kingdom. There will be famines and earthquakes in various places. All these things are the beginning of birth-pains (Matt. 24:4–8).

At the time of Jesus it was the height of the *pax Romana*, the world peace imposed by the Roman empire, so this turmoil that Jesus predicted was not actually taking place then, and did not begin for quite a long time. In recent years, though, the signs of the end of the world have become more and more frequent. There are now many, many cults, with their fake 'Messiahs'. Throughout the world there are wars on every continent, and nations are shaping up for war all the time. There are more wars now, and more devastating wars have taken place this century than at any other time in the history of the world.

According to United Nations statistics, more than one billion people are living in famine conditions. Despite the fact that the resources of the world are adequate to feed everyone, and despite advances in agricultural technology, a further one billion people are malnourished.

The United States Geological Survey Earthquake Report has some interesting and frightening statistics about earthquakes. Jesus prophesied that they would take place 'in various places', and one of the more significant things about earthquakes is that they are happening in places where they have never been known to happen before. And there are more of them. In the 1950s there were nine killer earthquakes; in the 1960s, thirteen; in the 1970s there were fifty-six; and in the 1980s a colossal seventy-four. If that trend continues, we can expect 125 serious earthquakes this decade.

You Have Been Warned!

The prophecies we have just mentioned are just a fraction of the predictions found in the Bible.

Most of them cluster around Jesus and the end of the world. You might think that if anyone made enough predictions, in vague enough terms, then some would be bound to come true. But if you look again at the sort of prophecies we've talked about in relation to Jesus, you will see that they are quite clear and definite. And if you look again at Jesus' predictions about the end of the world, you will see that he seems to know what will happen at the end more clearly, speaking in the first century, than we can now reliably predict, with all our sophisticated scientific equipment. Even if you aren't yet convinced about Jesus, you can see that the Bible has some very serious things to say about who Jesus is, and the world we live in. The probability of all these prophecies coming true just by human guess-work is too insignificant to be considered. God spoke through the prophets of old, so that we can be aware of his concern, of his loving plan for us and the world, and so that we know that he is in control.

TOMMY: The prophecies of the Bible are still coming true. There is no better time to come to God than now, because these prophecies are not intended to be depressing. Jesus says, after predicting the wars and so on, 'When these things begin to take place, stand up and lift up your heads, because your redemption is drawing near' (Luke 21:28).

BOBBY: That's true, Tommy, but answer me this: why are there so few men in heaven with beards?

TOMMY: I don't know, Bobby.

BOBBY: Because most men get in by a close shave!

TOMMY: How have we managed to survive all these years as comedians?!

BOBBY: Just one more!

TOMMY: No, please, Bobby! I can't stand the agony.

BOBBY: Who was the most popular actor in the Bible? Samson! He brought the house down! Okay, now back to the Bible.

How We Got Our Bible

All sorts of different people wrote the books of the Bible. There were at least forty different writers, and it was written in Hebrew, Aramaic and Greek. The books were written under all kinds of circumstances: Paul wrote from a Roman prison; John wrote the last book of the Bible from the Greek island of Patmos; most of the Old Testament was written in the ancient Near East, from Babylon to Israel.

From the time they were written, these books were regarded as special. In the time of Jesus and for long before, there was a professional class of people ('scribes') who were responsible for interpreting and preserving the special writings that became the Old Testament ('the Scriptures'). Their accuracy in copying the words is amazing. Not only would they read back what they had written, they would also count words and letters to ensure that nothing was missing. When the Dead Sea Scrolls of Isaiah, written before the birth of Jesus, were compared with a manuscript of the same book written a thousand years later, 95 per cent of the text was identical. All differences were insignificant in terms of the meaning of the book. And if you look at Isaiah, you'll see that it's quite a long book!

The Bible is not only found in the original languages. Because it is so important, it was translated into many others. There are some fine manuscripts of the Bible in Latin and some in Coptic. There are very occasional problems where the person translating didn't have the words, or didn't quite understand the phrase in the original. But once again, the level of accuracy is amazing. Not even the great works of Greek and Roman philosophy or history have been preserved so well, or so often, or so early. And when the Bible came to be translated into English, some of the translators like Tyndale paid with their lives for it, because the Bible is so radical a book and the authorities wanted to keep people ignorant of what it says.

Bible Morals

We've talked about what the Bible is. We've shown how carefully it has been preserved for centuries. We've given examples of how its prophecies have come true. We've seen how, for all the various writers and places it came from, it tells us about one God and his plans for the world. All these things show that the Bible is reliable, and that God was deeply involved in the process that ended in the book we have today. He wants to use it to change lives!

Now you can agree that the Bible is a remarkable book. You might even agree that it's supernatural. But where the rubber hits the road is where it shows us up for what we are. People like to say, 'I believe in the Sermon on the Mount', or 'I try to live by the Sermon on the Mount'. This is one of Jesus' sermons, recorded by Matthew (Matt. 5–7). Jesus says there, 'You have heard that it was said, "Do not commit adultery." But I tell you that anyone who looks at a woman lustfully has already committed adultery with her in his heart' (Matt. 5:27–28). This works for women, too, of course. We can live outwardly respectable lives, and nobody need know what we are thinking. But Jesus is radical! He says that the thoughts matter as well. God knows our thoughts, and we can't fool him that we always think kind, humble and pure thoughts.

The Sermon on the Mount turns all kinds of things on their heads. We like people to notice when we do good deeds, but Jesus tells us to do these things in secret if we want to please God (Matt. 6:1). We like to think that we are as good as most people and better than some. But Jesus says that's like trying to take a speck out of someone else's eye when you've got a log in your own (Matt. 7:3–5). We like to think that we're ready to put up with a lot of things, but there have to be limits! Jesus says that we should love our enemies (Matt. 5:44).

It's impossible to read the Sermon on the Mount seriously, and believe you can live by it without God. You can't read it seriously and say that it isn't true, because it picks out all our faults and follies and shows them as they are. But it isn't just about pointing out problems. The Bible is a book of answers, too. Jesus sums it all up when he says, 'I am the way and the truth and the life' (John 14:6). Being without God is like being lost, not knowing the truth (or living a lie), and being dead. Jesus says that through him we can know where we're going, face the truth about ourselves and God, and really live life to the full.

So, we believe the Bible is not only reliable – and there's plenty of evidence for that – but that it is also true; true in what it says about Jesus, true in what Jesus says about us through it. But you might be thinking, 'What right has Jesus to say these things? Why should I take any notice of some geezer from two thousand years ago?' We're going to look at Jesus and who he is in the next chapter, so read on! But before we leave this topic, you might want some help with reading the Bible.

Reading the Bible

If you've never tried it before the Bible can be a very difficult book to read. Probably the best place to start is the Gospels – Matthew, Mark, Luke and John. Luke is the easiest to understand. The Gospels are the centre, the core of the Bible, and they deal with Jesus' life, teaching, death and resurrection. Genesis, the first book of the Bible, tells some of the best stories of the Bible, and deals with the origins of the world and the Jewish nation. The psalms, in the middle, are lovely poems, Psalm 23 being the best known and most loved. The epistles (or letters), which follow the Gospels and Acts of the Apostles, tell individual churches how to live out the Christian faith in difficult circumstances. Romans is a letter from Paul, and there are many similarities between the problems faced by the Roman church, and those we face today.

God speaks through the Bible. If you feel you can, ask him to speak to you as you read it. If there's something you don't understand, either ask a Christian, or go to a Christian bookshop and ask for a simple guide to Bible reading, or perhaps a short commentary on the Bible book you are reading. Think about what you are reading, and ask yourself whether it tells you something about yourself or about God. You'll find that the more you learn, the more you want to know, and the more attractive God is.

Chapter 3

Who is Jesus?

Jesus Was a Real Human Being

No serious scholar doubts that Jesus lived at the time the Bible says he did. There are passages in the Jewish historian, Josephus, which refer to him, and Roman historians like Tacitus and Suetonius refer to Jesus and his followers. The Roman governor, Pliny, had to deal with Christians and kept writing to the emperor to ask advice and explain what he was doing (it wasn't very nice!). So we aren't relying solely on the Bible for information about Jesus' life.

Most of the detail comes from the Bible, though. We learn that Jesus was a descendant of Abraham and the great king of Israel, David. You carried your genealogy, the list of your ancestors, in your memory in those days as a kind of identity card, and Matthew records a version of Jesus' genealogy at the beginning of his Gospel so that readers will know where Jesus came from. Later in the Gospel, when Jesus' actions and teachings are beginning to amaze people, they all remind each other of who they think he is: 'Isn't this Joseph's son?' (Luke 4:22).

We know that Joseph was a tradesman, a carpenter by trade. As Jesus grew up, he would have learned the trade from Joseph, and got to know the properties of wood – how to cut it, what it was good for, the kinds of wood you use for different things. Jesus said once, 'Take my yoke upon you and learn from me . . . For my yoke is easy and my burden is light' (Matt. 11:29–30), and as an experienced carpenter, he would know how to make a yoke 'easy', comfortable, so that the oxen pulling a plough wouldn't get sore. He didn't live cut off from the realities of working life. He was used to working with his hands.

BOBBY: A bit more than you have for a long time, Tommy!

TOMMY: What are you talking about – I've carried you for the last thirty years!

BOBBY: That's cruel, Tommy.

TOMMY: But funny!

BOBBY: Okay, I agree.

TOMMY: Good. Now stop interrupting, some-one's trying to read this book.

Back to Jesus. We know something about Jesus as a boy (Luke 2:41–52). On one occasion, his family went to Jerusalem for a big festival when Jesus was twelve years old. When it was time for them all to go home, Jesus got left behind because he was talking with the scholars in the temple at Jerusalem. Mary and Joseph didn't worry about him, thinking he was with the other youths and families. But when they'd been travelling a whole day they realised he wasn't with them, and they had to go back to find him. When they found him he was discuss-ing deep things with the teachers of the temple and they were amazed at his understanding. This shows us not only that Jesus had an unusual grasp of religious matters, but also that he was a normal boy who normally ran off and played and went about with his friends. He didn't go around with a halo.

Jesus also had brothers. They didn't under-stand at first what he was doing, and once when Jesus was having a heated discussion with some religious leaders, they came to fetch him home.

Then Jesus' mother and brothers arrived. Standing outside, they sent someone in [to the house] to call him. A crowd was sitting around him, and they told him, 'Your mother and brothers are outside looking for you' . . . Then he looked at those seated in a circle around him and said, 'Here are my mother and my brothers! Whoever does God's will is my brother and sister and mother' (Mark 3:31–5).

In time, at least one of Jesus' brothers, James, became one of his followers and was killed for his belief. That must be one of the best arguments for the truth of Jesus' claims to be God. You can't hide what you really are from your own family!

At the start of his preaching career, Jesus experienced a particular time of temptation. The devil tried to tempt him to get popularity and power by spectacular tricks, like throwing himself off the highest building he knew and landing safely, or by turning stones into bread to feed the hungry. This last one was especially mean, because Jesus himself had had no food for forty days as part of his spiritual preparation for his ministry and he was hungry (Matt. 4:1–11). Jesus suffered hunger and loneliness and misery like the rest of us. His bodily needs and appetites were as real as ours. And he, too, was attracted by the thought of power and praise. But he didn't let his needs or appetites lead him into sin. That's where he was different from us, and that takes us on to the next section.

Jesus Was Much More than a Man

Jesus led a pretty normal life after the amazing events of his conception and birth, and before he started his preaching. We can pick up this much from all the Gospels. But the Gospels record Jesus going on to make astounding claims for himself. Not only that, but they also record that God did astounding things for him and through him. All these add up to the fact that Jesus was both man and God.

'How did Jesus claim to be God?' you might ask. We've already mentioned that there was a special word for God which is translated as 'LORD' in the Old Testament. This was the name that God called himself by when he spoke to Moses out of a burning bush. Moses faced a difficulty: God was asking him to go to the Pharaoh of Egypt and tell him to let his Israelite slaves go free. Not only that, but he was also asking Moses to lead the

Israelite people to a new land. Moses was a bit reluctant! So he says to God,

> 'Suppose I go to the Israelites and say to them, "The God of your fathers has sent me to you," and they ask me, "What is his name?" Then what shall I tell them?'
>
> God said to Moses, 'I AM WHO I AM. This is what you are to say to the Israelites: "I AM has sent me to you"' (Exod. 3:13–14).

So God's name is 'I AM'. Now one of Jesus' favourite kind of sayings was 'I am . . .' We've already mentioned 'I am the way and the truth and the life'. When he was in a discussion once, he claimed:

> 'Your father Abraham rejoiced at the thought of seeing my day; he saw it and was glad.'
>
> 'You are not yet fifty years old,' the Jews said to him, 'and you have seen Abraham!'
>
> 'I tell you the truth,' Jesus answered, 'before Abraham was born, I am!' At this, they picked up stones to stone him . . . (John 8:56–9).

We've seen that Jesus' genealogy has Abraham's name in it. But here, Jesus claims to have existed before Abraham, and by using the special name of God, he claims to be God too. The people knew exactly what he was saying, because they tried to stone him for blasphemy.

Nearly everybody who has ever considered the life of Jesus and his teaching has come to the conclusion that there was no contradiction between what Jesus taught and how he acted. In other words, he practised what he preached. He was incredibly humble. He loved kids and they loved him (and kids see through humbug faster than anyone). He cared for people, especially people nobody else bothered with – the lepers, the 'sinners', the lonely and those who were weak. Yet here he uses language that unmistakably claims divinity for himself. If he is wrong, then we've got problems: how can someone who is seriously deluded have come up with an example of living and teaching that is admired and respected the world over? What kind of people are we if the best ethical teaching we know comes from a nutter? If he's right, it shows that God is really like that! Loving, caring, humble, good with kids (and we're all kids at heart!) – an ideal Father!

Jesus knew he was going to be killed. He believed the prophecies about the servant of God who would suffer and die, and he knew he was the one who would fulfil those prophecies. Just as he was being arrested, at the time when most of us would be wound up and ready to run or fight, he was calm and able to show real love. One of his followers pulled out a sword and cut off the ear of the high priest's servant (Luke 22:50). Most probably it was Peter who did this, and he was so wound up, he couldn't even aim straight. But Jesus said 'No more of this!' and he touched the man's ear and healed him. He cared about this man, who had come to take him away. And he cared about Peter, knowing that he was impulsive and might do something he would regret.

Miracles

Jesus performed many miracles, and there were miracles at his birth, too. He healed people of terrible diseases, and even raised people from the dead. He rose from the dead himself, and we'll think more about that in a minute. There are different ways you can come to terms with these miracles. You can say one of two things: either miracles happen, or they don't. The common-sense view is that they do, because 'miracle' means (among other things) something that can't be explained by what we already know.

We say things like, 'It was a miracle I escaped unhurt' from, say, a car crash. And we mean that anybody in that situation would have expected to be seriously injured. We probably all know people who have 'miraculously' got better from illness, and the doctors have been quite unable to explain why it should be so. To say miracles can't happen, on the other hand, is to express an absolute faith in something that can never be proved. Christians might well envy such strength of faith! It is an assumption, not, as it might seem at first sight, an argument.

Jesus could perform miracles pretty much at will. He was tempted by the devil to do tricks. But the tricks the devil tempted him to do were against his nature: instead of providing bread to gain popularity, Jesus spoke of himself as the 'bread of life', the one who can give spiritual satisfaction (John 6:35. Notice that Jesus says again, 'I *am* the bread of life.') Instead of doing a death-defying dive from the high point of the temple building to amaze people, Jesus gave his life to save them. The kind of miracles he did showed what kind of person he was. John calls them 'signs' because they point to his nature as God. He is in control of the natural world, he has power over disease, he wants people to respond to him.

Take just one example:

Some men brought to him a paralytic, lying on a mat. When Jesus saw their faith, he said to the paralytic, 'Take heart, son; your sins are forgiven.'

At this, some of the teachers of the law said to themselves, 'This fellow is blaspheming!'

Knowing their thoughts, Jesus said, 'Why do you entertain evil thoughts in your hearts? Which is easier: to say, "Your sins are forgiven," or to say, "Get up and walk"? But so that you may know that the Son of Man has authority on earth to forgive sins . . .' Then he said to the paralytic, 'Get up, take your mat and go home.' And the man got up and went home. When the crowd saw this, they were filled with awe; and they praised God, who had given such authority to men (Matt. 9:2–8).

Three things stand out from this account. One, Jesus was dealing with people, not just pulling rabbits from a hat for fun. He saw the faith of the man's friends and he responded to them, and, in the process, to those who thought you shouldn't say the sort of things Jesus said.

Two, he shows that some things are more important than health, and indeed, more difficult to come by: forgiveness in Jesus' book was worth dying for. Three, it shows Jesus' authority, which even the crowd who didn't necessarily believe in him recognised as from God. So miracles show who Jesus is and what kind of person he was. They didn't happen randomly, but Jesus did them for definite reasons. Above all, he did them because, as God, he could, and wanted to, because he had compassion on people.

Jesus' Death

Jesus' death and resurrection are the most important part of the discussion of who Jesus is. The facts about Jesus' death are clear, because crucifixion was one of the commoner forms of execution used by the Romans. The aim was to draw out the dying and to humiliate the victim, as a kind of warning to anyone who might be thinking about defying the Roman government.

Actually, it was not the Roman government that was upset by Jesus. Pontius Pilate, the governor of the province, tried to set Jesus free when the Jewish leaders brought him before

Pilate for sentencing. He repeatedly said that he saw no reason why Jesus should be sentenced to death. But the crowd that had gathered for the Passover festival, roused by the enemies of Jesus, shouted Pilate down. He was afraid of a riot, so he gave in.

Jesus was taken away and scourged. The scourge was a kind of whip with lead shot or bits of bone in the thongs, and it ripped the flesh. People sometimes died under the scourge. Then Jesus was mocked. One of the titles for the Messiah was 'King of the Jews', so they put royal purple robes on Jesus and pretended to honour him. They crowned him with thorns instead of a crown. Then he was forced to carry his own cross, the beam to which he would be nailed, to the place of execution. He was so exhausted from the torture he had already been through that he could not carry it for long. So a man called Simon from Cyrene in North Africa was compelled to carry the cross. He had probably done nothing wrong. He just happened to be in the wrong place at the wrong time, and he was black.

When the procession reached Golgotha, 'the place of the skull', Jesus was stretched on the cross and nailed to it. This was where it needed the skills of a professional executioner, because if the nails went in the wrong place, they could cut an artery and shorten the victim's sufferings. That would defeat the object of the exercise. Once nailed, the cross beam was lifted up into place. Then the victim had either to hang from his hands to take the weight from his feet, which made it difficult to breathe, or he had to push down on the spiked feet to take his breath. All this in the heat of the sun and with flies attracted by the blood. Usually, it took the victim between a day and three days to die, slowly and in exquisite agony.

A Different Death?

In many ways Jesus' death was no different from the hundreds who died in the same fashion at the hands of the Romans. Two other men were crucified with him for murder and plotting against the government. One used his last breaths to curse, and to abuse Jesus. But the other, in one of those moments of vision that come in terrible crises, realised that though he was guilty of crime, Jesus wasn't. There were probably groups of people around who had been looking for a figurehead to lead a revolt against the Romans, and doubtless Jesus had been

considered for the role. These men might have
known a lot about Jesus for this very reason:

> One of the criminals who hung there hurled
> insults at him: 'Aren't you the Christ? Save
> yourself and us!'
>
> But the other criminal rebuked him.
> 'Don't you fear God,' he said, 'since you
> are under the same sentence? We are pun-
> ished justly, for we are getting what our
> deeds deserve. But this man has done noth-
> ing wrong.'
>
> Then he said, 'Jesus, remember me when
> you come into your kingdom.'
>
> Jesus answered him, 'I tell you the truth,
> today you will be with me in paradise' (Luke
> 23:39–43).

In extremity, this man reached out for God, and
found him hanging on the cross beside him. As a
political saviour Jesus had been rejected, but
now the terrorist found a true saviour for his
soul. This man knew that Jesus was different,
and that Jesus' death was different.

Just after this episode, at about midday, it
became dark and Jesus cried out in horror and
desperation, 'My God, my God, why have you
forsaken me?' Even the Roman centurion in

charge of the crucifixion recognised that Jesus was not guilty: 'Surely,' he said, 'this was a righteous man' (Luke 23:47). But from what Jesus cried out, and from the darkness, God was making it clear that Jesus was being cut off. He had done nothing wrong, but was being treated by God and by men as if he was guilty of anything and everything. He was 'bearing our sins', being punished for things that he had not done, but that *we*, the human race, have done; evil things that we still do against each other and against God. Jesus had become the filth that is our sin, and God cut off the very sight of him.

He died forgiving those who put him there. 'Father, forgive them, for they do not know what they are doing' (Luke 23:34). He died at about three o'clock in the afternoon, and when the soldiers came to clear things up by breaking the legs of the victims, they found Jesus was already dead. A soldier thrust a spear into his side, and blood and water came out. This indicates death, because at death, the blood separates into a clear liquid like water, and the red mass of blood cells. Before dark, the bodies were taken down from the crosses, and Jesus' body was taken to be buried by a man from Arimathea called Joseph. The body was wrapped in strips of linen after being washed, and quantities of myrrh and aloes were wrapped in with the linen strips. This was a kind of preservative. The body was then put in Joseph of Arimathea's own tomb, and it was sealed up and guarded by the authorities.

The tomb was sealed by a large stone across the entrance. Possibly there was some other seal in addition. Certainly there was a guard of Roman soldiers, highly trained and disciplined men, who knew that if they failed in their duty, they could be executed. So that was the end of the story: a good man unjustly, but very effectively, silenced. Or so the authorities thought.

The End?

But Jesus didn't stay dead. He was raised by God from the dead, and there were lots of people who saw him alive again afterwards. The tomb was empty, and though they must have wanted to, the authorities could not find the body of Jesus and put an end to all the ferment that was going on among his followers. Women went to the tomb early on the day after the festival, but found it empty. The guards had probably left to report the same thing. Mary Magdalene went to fetch Peter, and he went there, went inside the tomb and saw the linen strips lying where Jesus' body had been. It was at this point that things started to fall into place in the minds of Jesus' followers. They had been bitterly disappointed when Jesus was crucified, they had abandoned him to save themselves, and afterwards they even thought about going back to their old jobs. But when they saw the empty tomb, and when they saw Jesus himself alive, they started to understand what he had been telling them all along: that he had to die, but that he would rise again.

Some Theories of the Resurrection

According to many historians, the resurrection is one of the best-attested facts of history. But of course there are many alternative theories which try to explain it away. There are several theories that suggest different groups of people snatched the body. The Jewish leaders did it so that the followers of Jesus couldn't do it and claim that Jesus had risen. Jesus' followers did it so that they *could* claim that Jesus had risen. The Romans did it so that neither of the others could. Or of course, the body was put in the wrong tomb – both the Romans and Joseph of Arimathea somehow got muddled and put the body in somebody else's tomb.

Now there are lots of specific problems with all of these theories. But the major one is that *none* of these groups would be interested in body-snatching. Once someone is dead, they are dead. Hard-headed Romans knew that their executioner didn't make mistakes; depressed and terrified followers of Jesus only wanted to lie low and keep out of the way; religious Jewish people would never touch a dead body except by accident or duty, because it would make them ritually unclean. Nobody else in history has the same sort of far-fetched theories to explain their continuing activity in the world after they are dead!

Oh, yes, and there's the theory that Jesus wasn't really dead, but revived in the coolness of the tomb, pushed back the stone over the entrance with his smashed wrists, and ran off on his impaled feet, having somehow got past the guards. And then he persuaded his followers that he had risen again by somehow sneaking into a room with a locked door. Please!

Several people have set out to disprove the reality of the resurrection. Lew Wallace and his friend Robert Ingersoll decided they would study all the evidence and write a book that would prove it was all a myth. At an early stage in the writing of the book, Lew Wallace found himself on his knees crying out to Jesus. He was utterly convinced by the evidence that Jesus was the Son of God. The book he wrote turned into the great novel, *Ben Hur*.

Another writer was Frank Morrison. He set out with the same end in mind: to prove, given the limits of historical investigation, that Jesus did not rise again. He too was convinced after a little while that it was true. His book, *Who Moved the Stone?* is still in print. It's a detailed argument exploring all the possibilities, and one of the best books you can read on the resurrection (after the Bible, of course!). What all this goes to show is that ignorance is more of a problem than evidence! If you are unsure about what we're saying, the best thing to do is find out.

The Significance of the Resurrection

Perhaps it's the significance of the resurrection that makes it hard to swallow. If Jesus just died, then we can respect him as a good man, but his teaching, and his claims about himself, can be quietly ignored. He would be as significant perhaps as Plato, whose writings we've all been reading, haven't we? But if Jesus rose again from the dead, then he has unique authority to tell us what matters in God's terms, in eternity. The resurrection shows that God underwrites Jesus' claims. And more, that we can know God now, through Jesus, just as his followers did two thousand years ago. The Bible says that the amazing power that raised Jesus from the dead is available to, and at work in, the lives of those who believe in him.

Peter, the very man who ran away from Jesus and denied that he knew him when it came to the crunch, later wrote this about Jesus:

> He committed no sin, and no deceit was found in his mouth. When they hurled their insults at him, he did not retaliate; when he suffered, he made no threats. Instead, he entrusted himself to him who judges justly. He himself bore our sins in his body on the tree, so that we might die to sins and live for righteousness; by his wounds you have been healed (1 Peter 2:22–4).

Peter says that through Jesus' death we can be saved or healed. Through Jesus, we can be made into the sort of person Jesus was and is. The process is one of death and resurrection: Jesus takes our evil to the cross with him; with him, the sin and evil is put to death; and we get to be so radically renewed that it is like rising from the dead. This is what salvation means.

Writing to the church in the city of Colossae, Paul says the same kind of things:

> Since, then, you have been raised with Christ, set your hearts on things above, where Christ is seated at the right hand of God. Set your minds on things above, not on earthly things. For you died, and your life is now hidden with Christ in God (Col. 3:1–3).

This is the next step, if you like. Dying to sin, and being raised to new life is what has already happened to the people Paul is writing to. Now they have to do their part to sustain their life. We'll say more about spiritual growth later. You can see, though, that because Jesus was raised from the dead, Christians have a new kind of life. The resurrection is not just a curiosity of history, it has real impact on life here and now (and in the future).

Jesus Now

Because God raised Jesus, we know that he is alive. But he wasn't just raised to go on living an ordinary life and having to die later on. After he was raised, he spent some time with his followers, eating with them, teaching them, letting them touch him. Once he even appeared to about five hundred people (1 Cor. 15:6). This was important for them and for us, because they needed to know that he was real. They also needed to know that he would not always be physically with them, but with them in a new way. At the end of this period, which lasted about six weeks, he was taken to heaven (Acts 1:9). Before he left, he promised them power, spiritual power through the Holy Spirit. All who believe in Jesus are given the Holy Spirit, who works powerfully in their lives to enable them to live for Jesus and like Jesus. He is Jesus' parting promise and gift to his church (Acts 1:5, 8).

One of the earliest Christian statements of belief was 'Jesus is Lord'. That got people into trouble because Caesar thought he was lord! When we call Jesus 'Lord', we mean that he has the right to direct our lives, just as a lord of the realm has the right to direct his servants. He has the authority (Matt. 28:18). We submit our lives to him, because as our Lord and God he knows what is best for us. We ask for the Holy Spirit's guidance in decisions and dilemmas we face.

But even though he is Lord, he has not lost any of the characteristics which are so attractive. He is still humble (now that's amazing!): he doesn't force himself on us. He is still loving, caring for the weak and the underprivileged. He knows what it's like to feel like us: he still knows what it's like to suffer, to be tempted, to be mocked. He promises to be with us in these things, and to put our case before his Father. In this he acts like a high priest did in the Jewish worship, taking a sacrifice before God on behalf of the people. One of the letters in the Bible, written to an early Jewish Christian church, put it like this:

Since we have a great high priest who has gone through the heavens, Jesus the Son of God, let us hold firmly to the faith we profess. For we do not have a high priest who is unable to sympathise with our weaknesses, but we have one who has been tempted in every way, just as we are – yet was without sin. Let us then approach the throne of grace with confidence, so that we may receive mercy and find grace to help us in our time of need (Heb. 4:14–16).

There's so much more we could say. We could tell you of people who have been healed by Jesus, people who have been transformed completely, people who have been released from addiction to drugs or sex, people who have been freed from hatred and fear, people who have given their lives for others, people who have worked selflessly for the good of others. These are all people who been able to say 'Jesus is Lord', and have shown it in their lives.

Some Testimonies

BOBBY: We've been pretty serious for a while now, because this is important stuff. Let me tell you that when I was running around drinking and womanising I never gave Jesus a thought. The cross was just a thing you saw in church, something meaningless. It was only when I reached rock bottom, when my life and my marriage were falling apart that I realised I needed help. A man told me about Jesus, and when I got on my knees and asked him to forgive me, I understood. Now he's like the best brother in the world to me! I can tell him everything. He doesn't mind me telling him my troubles, in fact he helps me get through them. He isn't a figment of someone's imagination, he's alive today.

TOMMY: I had a very vague belief in God, and I thought we'd all end up in heaven. But that kind of belief did me no good. It didn't stop me doing exactly what I wanted and ending up miserable. It didn't help me when my mother was dying, even though I prayed to the 'something' I thought might have been out there. I blamed God at the same time. It's funny how God always crops up when there's a crisis, or we need a scapegoat. Why are 'acts of God' in insurance policies always horrible things? I suppose 'acts of the devil' doesn't sound quite right, even though it might be truer.

But as soon as I reached out for Jesus the Lord, I found he was there. Now I plan my life around him. When Bobby and I meet to decide things, we always discuss it with Jesus too. He's our friend. I couldn't manage without him: he gives me strength and encouragement every day of my life.

Philip Schaff, a great historian, wrote this:

Jesus of Nazareth, without money or arms, conquered more millions than Alexander, Caesar, Mohammed and Napoleon; without science and learning, he shed more light on things human and divine than all the scholars and philosophers combined; without the eloquence of the school, he spoke words of life such as were never spoken before, nor since, and produced effects that lie beyond the reach of the orator or poet. Without writing a single line, he has set more pens in motion and furnished themes for sermons, orations, discussions, works of art, learned volumes, and sweet songs of praise than the whole army of great men of ancient and modern times. Born in a manger and crucified as a malefactor, he now controls the destinies of the civilized world and runs a spiritual empire which embraces one-third of the inhabitants of the globe.

To finish the chapter with the Bible, we will quote one of the loveliest passages about Jesus in the New Testament. This brings us back to who Jesus is. It was probably used as a hymn in the early church, and it summarises what we believe:

[Jesus], being in very nature God, did not consider equality with God something to be grasped, but made himself nothing, taking the very nature of a servant, being made in human likeness.

And being found in appearance as a man, he humbled himself and became obedient to death – even death on a cross!

Therefore God exalted him to the highest place and gave him the name that is above every name, that at the name of Jesus every knee should bow, in heaven and on earth and under the earth, and every tongue confess that Jesus Christ is Lord, to the glory of God the Father (Phil. 2:6–11).

Chapter 4

Why Come to God?

Why Don't We?

There are many good reasons why we should come to God. There are no good reasons why we shouldn't. So why don't we? Well, sometimes we have wrong ideas about God, and perhaps we blame him for the pain in our lives. Or we don't want to change, because God seems to threaten our way of life and our comfort. Or we just think we're okay as we are.

You may be suffering from the loss of a loved one, perhaps through death or divorce, and it's easy to blame God for that. Perhaps someone has hurt you deeply and you feel that God might be the same, and he is the last thing you need. We all tend to feel that God should do something about suffering if he loves us so much.

You may be doing wrong things, and you

don't want God just now. But believe us, we have done plenty of wrong things, and we now wish we had turned to God earlier. That way, we would have had the fulfilled lives that we have now, rather than the shallow lives that went with selfishness and keeping God out. Perhaps you feel that you can't stop what you are doing. But it is possible. God can forgive you for the wrong things, and help you start again.

You may be saying, 'Well, I'm not that bad really.' Or 'I go out of my way to help people, and I wouldn't hurt anybody.' Or you might be saying, 'I say my prayers, I don't think I'm what you would call a sinner.' But we know how easy it is to kid ourselves.

BOBBY: I used to think I was okay! There I was, doing everything bad there was – committing adultery, being greedy and violent, and much more, but I still thought, 'I'm not doing anybody any harm, I'm helping people out in my own way, and I make people laugh, so I can't be all that bad really.' That's how I used to think.

TOMMY: It's a long time since he made me laugh! (Only joking, Bobby.) Like Bobby, I didn't think I was too bad either. I was doing the same kind of wrong things. And I was fooling myself, too. I told myself I was only doing what everybody else does, and then I would do the odd good turn for somebody, and I was satisfied that I wasn't at all bad.

We all think these things. Pain and bitterness can keep us away from God. Doing wrong things keeps us away from God. Feeling that we are as good as anybody else can keep us away from God. But these things are all to do with looking at ourselves. If we are to come to God, we need to think about him too. So let's investigate for a minute what the Bible means when it says, 'Jesus died on the cross so that our sins may be forgiven.'

What Is God Like?

We've already explained what God is like, to some extent. He's like Jesus. But we want to explain it a bit more, to help you understand what God was doing in sending Jesus. Basically, God sent Jesus to die on the cross so that our sins may be forgiven. This is both strange and familiar. You've heard it before. So have we, and the more we hear it, the better it sounds. But it's strange as well, and we need to explain it.

In Old Testament times (that's the time before Jesus in the land of Israel), people used to sacrifice animals to atone for their sins. They would offer the animal to God because they had done something wrong against him, or against someone else. By killing the animal, they showed they knew how serious the wrongdoing was (it was a matter of life and death); and by offering the sacrifice to God, they showed they realised that every sin is sin against God. They knew that God is holy – that is, perfect, pure and good. And they knew that both deliberately and by accident they were not. All the ritual surrounding sacrifice is described in the book of Leviticus, and it might seem a bit strange to us. But underneath it all there is the need for people to find peace with God through having their sins forgiven.

Often the sacrifice offered to God was a lamb. Right at the beginning of John's Gospel, John the Baptist saw Jesus and pointed him out, and said, 'Look, the Lamb of God, who takes away the sin of the world' (John 1:29). What John meant was that Jesus would be killed as a sacrifice, just like the animals were, so that we could be forgiven for our wrongdoing. Jesus was special, though, as we've said. If you imagine that your wealth is counted in the number of sheep you have, then you can see that a lamb represents a certain part of your wealth. Sacrificing one costs you. If then you think that God sacrificed his 'lamb', his only Son, so that *we* could be forgiven, you see how much it cost him, and how much he wants us to have peace with him. Jesus was God's total sacrifice for us, and as a result we no longer have to sacrifice animals. When we accept what Jesus has done for us, we can know that God forgives us, and we can live with him and enjoy his love. That's what we mean when we say that Jesus died on the cross so that our sins can be forgiven.

So that's what God is like. He is holy and powerful, but also unbelievably loving. As soon as you start to think about God as he really is, you also start to realise how imperfect you are. When you look at God, it feels a bit silly to say, 'I'm not really that bad.' We have all got secrets, things that we're ashamed of, things that we don't want anyone else to know about. We don't even live up to our own standards, let alone God's! The Bible tells it like it really is: immorality, greed, lust, wrongful thoughts, envy, anger . . . (see for example, Col. 3:5–8, and Eph. 5:3–9). If you can read these passages and say truthfully that you aren't guilty of any of these things, then put the book down, and thank you for reading this far! But we will just about guarantee that one or another of these sins is your problem, just as they are ours. The answer is not going to church, or reading the Bible, or having theological debates, but turning to God and asking him for forgiveness through his Son, Jesus. Then these things that we've just mentioned make sense.

What's Stopping Us?

We said earlier that pain, or sin, or feeling satisfied with ourselves can all keep us away from God. But once you start thinking about what God is like (and we've already said a lot about that), you can see that these are very good reasons for coming to God.

Because Jesus suffered rejection and betrayal and both physical and emotional pain, he knows what you are going through if you are suffering. He can share the pain with you in a way that no-one else can. And he can take away the bitterness from your heart, and fill you with love; he can take away the emptiness you feel and give your life meaning.

No-one wants suffering. But sometimes we enjoy sin, so we tend to hold on to it. You can't hold on to sin and seriously come to God, because God is holy. But if you want to break the hold that sin has over you, so that you don't have to do things that you regret or feel ashamed of, then God will do it if you come to him.

One of the things that we hold on to most tightly is the idea that we are okay, even when we know there are secrets and shames in our lives. Only God can give us true confidence that we are okay. He does this not by pretending that it doesn't matter what we've done, and the kind of people we've become, but by forgiving us.

BOBBY: Let me try and explain it this way. Say you're thirsty, and standing in front of you is a glass of water. You can imagine what the water would taste like, and the satisfying feeling it would give you as it went down. You can imagine the enjoyment of not feeling desperately thirsty any more. But it is only when you reach out and drink the water that it all happens. Until then, it's all in your imagination. Coming to God and asking him into our lives gives us the experience of our needs being met, our emptiness being filled, and not having that constant niggle that we're fooling ourselves that we're okay. Just like the drink, it tastes good, too!

TOMMY: Bobby is right for once!

BOBBY: For once! Thanks, Tommy.

TOMMY: You're welcome. If you'd asked me a few years ago if I was going to become a Christian, I'd have said, 'No way!' But once I started thinking about God, I realised I needed him, and asked him into my life. I had a life filled with pain and sin and self-satisfaction – I had the lot! But I had to come to him, and now I only wish I'd turned to him sooner.

God's Special Offer

God is generous, and he makes us all a very special offer. It costs us nothing. You've probably had the experience of going round the New Year sales (in mid-November, as they get earlier and earlier!) and snapping up things that seem to be really good value. Only to find you could have got them cheaper somewhere else, or that they weren't worth the money in the first place. Well, God's special offer won't disappoint. He offers us new life, forgiveness, and his constant friendship and guidance. But as we've said, he doesn't force his offer on anyone.

God has given us free will. He has given us choice. What we ought to know is what the alternatives are, and Paul puts them very plainly:

> If you live according to the sinful nature, you will die; but if by the Spirit you put to death the misdeeds of the body, you will live, for those who are led by the Spirit of God are sons of God (Rom. 8:13).

Boy, that's a radical statement! But it's simple and straightforward – you don't have to be a theological genius to see what he means. We can live according to our basic instincts and appetites and die, or we can live according to God's Spirit and live with him forever.

TOMMY: I lived according to my basic instincts. Lust, greed, selfishness all came naturally to me. I didn't really know how to be different. I didn't know you *could* be different consistently, and not just on Christmas Day or a special occasion! What God did was to change my nature and give me a new life with different instincts. It was so radical, it was like being born again. Whoops! Now I've said it, and you'll be putting the book down thinking, 'I don't want to get into this.' Well, hold on a minute! We both used to think

'Born again Christians' were a cult or something. At any rate, we thought they were the sort of people to avoid at all costs! How incredibly ignorant we were! While I'm on the subject, I used to think that anyone who went to church wanted to be a do-gooder, and had nothing better to get on with. Wrong!

Being Born Again

This has become a kind of label, so perhaps we'd better get behind the label to the truth. One night a man came to see Jesus. He was pretty important, being one of the members of the Jewish kind of parliament, so he was embarrassed to be seen visiting Jesus. His name was Nicodemus, and he started by being very polite to Jesus. But Jesus got straight to the point. This is how John tells the story:

Now there was a man of the Pharisees named Nicodemus, a member of the Jewish ruling council. He came to Jesus at night and said, 'Rabbi, we know you are a teacher who has come from God. For no-one could perform the miraculous signs you are doing if God were not with him.'

In reply Jesus declared, 'I tell you the truth, no-one can see the kingdom of God unless he is born again' (John 3:1–3).

Nicodemus was a decent sort of bloke. He lived a moral life. He believed in God. He didn't want to dismiss Jesus without giving him a chance. But instead of him interviewing Jesus for the role of Nice Guy, he finds Jesus interviewing him. They spend some time talking about what being born again means, because Nicodemus didn't understand any more than we did. What Jesus was saying was that no matter how decent, no matter how important, no matter how kind we are, we still need to be transformed by God, and enter his kingdom by accepting Jesus as Lord. Jesus gave Nicodemus the alternatives:

God so loved the world that he gave his one and only Son, that whoever believes in him shall not perish but have eternal life. For God did not send his Son into the world to condemn the world, but to save the world through him. Whoever believes in him is not condemned, but whoever does not believe stands condemned already because he has not believed in the name of God's one and only Son. This is the verdict: Light has come into the world, but men loved darkness instead of light because their deeds were evil (John 3:16–19).

BOBBY: I understand this now, but before I became a Christian I didn't really have a clue what it meant. One of the things it means is that no-one can know God as he is unless they have a personal relationship with him through Jesus. I used to believe in God. In my hippy days, I thought Jesus was a spaceman who had been sent to earth by a superior being! I certainly believed there was something out there. But I still had to be born again.

TOMMY: Like millions of people today, I'd have answered 'Yes' if you'd asked me if I believed in God. I didn't know, but I felt pretty sure there was a God. But if you'd asked me if I wanted to meet him, I'd have run a mile! I thought you only had to meet God when you were dead. And because the prospect of meeting God face to face was so frightening, I invented my own beliefs about him. I convinced myself that I would do enough good deeds to guarantee me a place in heaven. Now, you didn't think I was that stupid, did you?

BOBBY: I did! He once went to the dog track and bet on the rabbit!

TOMMY: That's an old joke, Bobby.

BOBBY: I'm an old comedian, Tommy! Like Tommy, I would have been desperately afraid of meeting God. Sure, I could drink and fight with the best of them, but when it came to God, I was a pathetic coward. And since I have become a Christian I've talked with lots of people about God. People have come up with every conceivable theory about what God is like, but at the end of the debate when I have asked them to pray with me and come face to face with God, they've declined. Funny, isn't it? We can all talk and theorise about God, but we are desperately frightened of him, and want to keep him 'out there'. Only as a vague idea, with no importance for life. But the truth is that to have real life, we have to come to God and start again. We have to meet him face to face.

Eternal Life

Jesus told Nicodemus that everyone who believes in him will have eternal life. There are lots of jokes about people sitting around on clouds playing harps, and getting into heaven by the pearly gate, and fooling St Peter. But we're not going to tell them for now!

The thing about eternal life is that it starts now. When you are born again, you start living a new life that goes on forever. It's imperfect now, but when you go through death to be with Jesus, it becomes perfect. That's why the idea that we're all going to sit around playing harps for ever and ever and get bored out of our minds is wrong. Jesus said about his followers, 'I have come that they may have life, and have it to the full' (John 10:10). Later he said, 'I give them eternal life, and they shall never perish; no-one shall snatch them out of my hand' (John 10:28). The relationship with Jesus that we start now goes on, and we shall never get tired of being with him and will always enjoy his love.

We don't know very much about heaven, except that it's the place to be, and will be very nice! We know what won't be there, and we know that we will be with God. John had a vision in which he saw some marvellous things, and this is how he speaks of heaven:

I heard a loud voice from the throne saying, 'Now the dwelling of God is with men, and he will live with them. They will be his people, and God himself will be with them and be their God. He will wipe every tear from their eyes. There will be no more death or mourning or crying or pain, for the old order of things has passed away' (Rev. 21:3–4).

This is all part of the special offer that God makes to us. We won't find a better offer anywhere. We receive all this when we have faith in Jesus.

Faith

We'll look in more depth at faith later. We've already said that faith in God is not automatic, it has to be something that we *do*, an act of will. Sometimes, though, we have faith that is more or less automatic, and it isn't in God. We say, 'I don't need God, I'm financially secure'; or, 'I'm happy as I am, and I don't feel any need for God'; or, 'I don't want to change things, lots of other people manage without religion.' These things are expressions of faith. We are putting our trust in money, or feelings, or other people's opinions.

You don't have to be an accountant to know

that money is only temporary. There have been so many booms and crashes in recent years, you can hardly tell which is which. Jesus warned that it was difficult for wealthy people to get to heaven, because money gives a false sense of security. You can't take money with you when you die, and if you have the true wealth of knowing Jesus, no-one can take it from you, whether you've got money or not. You can invest your life in money, or invest your life in things that will last. Faith in money is a very poor option.

Feeling happy isn't a very good guide to the truth. Drugs can produce a feeling of happiness. So can disease: there is a stage in some terrible conditions where the person feels elated. We need to seek the truth for our lives, not just feelings. Feelings can help us know that we need help, as Bobby has said was the case with him. But if what we are saying about God is true, then everybody needs to come to Jesus, however they feel. Having faith in feelings isn't very sensible. How long will you feel completely happy?

We don't trust other people's opinions about almost anything, so why religion? How many times has someone told you that a certain food is out of this world, or a film is the best one you've ever seen, and you've found both really disappointing, or even unpleasant? The creatures we associate with this kind of blind faith are lemmings and sheep. Say no more! If other people want to just drift with the tide, there's no reason why you should.

The fact is that having faith in these other things is unbelief in God. Unbelief cuts us off from God and the things that he wants to give us. Above all, he wants to give us himself, and the security of knowing him for eternity. But he also wants to give us what we need for our lives, physically, financially, emotionally and in our relationships. Jesus said,

Do not worry, saying, 'What shall we eat?' or 'What shall we drink?' or 'What shall we wear?' For the pagans run after all these things, and your heavenly Father knows that you need them. But seek first his kingdom and his righteousness, and all these things will be given to you as well. Therefore do not worry about tomorrow, for tomorrow will worry about itself. Each day has enough trouble of its own (Matt. 6:31–4).

BOBBY: Unbelief causes all sorts of fears and

insecurity. Everything good our hearts long for, God wants to give us. And this can happen if we have faith.

TOMMY: Rejoice, readers! Bobby is finally getting a brain! (Just another of my little jokes, folks.)

BOBBY: That's exactly what it was – little!

TOMMY: Thank you, Bobby! Faith starts with need, and once you want to know God and be forgiven by him, then faith begins to grow. Jesus said even the smallest grain of faith, like a tiny seed, could grow into something big like a tree. That's a picture of how, when we start to rely on God, our faith stops being tiny and grows to involve the whole of our life. It takes over from these false faiths that we've been talking about, that we've all relied on at some stage, and gives us real security in life.

So Why Come to God?

If we come back to where we started this chapter, we can answer that question. There are many good reasons why we should come to God. He loves us, he offers us new life and security for eternity. There are no good reasons why we shouldn't come to God, only bad ones! So in our next chapter, we're gong to talk about how we come to God.

Chapter 5

Coming to God

Faith Again!

Coming to God involves faith. You might be thinking, 'I haven't got enough faith' or 'I haven't got that kind of faith'. But it's not as if you suddenly find extra bits of faith hidden somewhere in your pocket or purse, and then you've got enough. Nor is it that faith is believing impossible things. So it isn't out of reach for ordinary people, and as we've said already, it is something that can grow once it is exercised. So let's take a look at some examples of faith.

A Woman Is Healed

There's a very simple story in Mark's Gospel. It's almost hidden in a longer and more detailed account of how Jesus healed the daughter of an important Jewish leader. Jesus is just going off to the leader's house:

A large crowd followed and pressed around him. And a woman was there who had been subject to bleeding for twelve years. She had suffered a great deal under the care of many doctors and had spent all she had, yet instead of getting better she grew worse. When she heard about Jesus, she came up behind him in the crowd and touched his cloak, because she thought, 'If I just touch his clothes, I will be healed.' Immediately her bleeding stopped and she felt in her body that she was freed from her suffering.

At once Jesus realised that power had gone out from him. He turned around in the crowd and asked, 'Who touched my clothes?'

'You see the people crowding against you,' his disciples answered, 'and yet you can ask, "Who touched me?"'

But Jesus kept looking around to see who had done it. Then the woman, knowing what had happened to her, came and fell at his feet and, trembling with fear, told him the whole truth. He said to her,

'Daughter, your faith has healed you. Go in peace and be freed from your suffering' (Mark 5:24–34).

In the Jewish law, a woman's bleeding made her unclean. So this woman would have been unable to take any part in the social and religious life of her community. She would not have been able to touch anybody without making them unclean and unable to attend the temple worship. She would have been practically an outcast. She had done everything she could to sort out the problem, and had only got worse. But she had faith. She went to Jesus, and you can imagine that she must have had to push her way through the crowd without worrying what people said or thought. Her eyes were fixed on Jesus. She had an absolute determination to get through to him. Her faith was centred on Jesus to the extent that she only wanted to touch his clothes. She didn't want to engage him in conversation, discuss her symptoms, or even go with him to witness a miracle. All she knew was that he was the one who could meet her need.

Jesus did meet her need. She was healed. But faith is never impersonal, and Jesus knew that something had happened to him in the press of the crowd. He was drawn to her, just as, by faith, she had drawn healing from him. Of course the woman was scared. Not only was she afraid that she had made Jesus unclean, she was awed by the fact that she had been healed – she might even have felt she had cheated in getting her healing like that! Jesus kindly and quietly confirmed her faith and her healing, and sent her on her way in peace.

It was the woman's faith that led to her healing. It was her faith that made her different from the crowd. Her faith basically consisted of two things: her need for healing, and her conviction that Jesus could meet that need.

An Old Testament Example of Faith

Noah was a good man in a bad world. God told him quite simply that he was going to clean up the world by flooding it out. And Noah had to build a massive ship to keep alive the various species of land animals. Now God gave Noah a lot of instructions about how to make the boat (Gen. 6:14–16). These included the kind of wood, the size, how many decks, and so on. This suggests that Noah had never built a ship before, and he might well have lived inland. You can imagine, in any case, what the neighbours would say: 'Nutcase Noah', 'ark at him', 'water on the brain', and so on. The Bible just says, 'Noah did everything just as God had commanded him' (Gen. 6:22; 7:5).

Noah's faith was different from the woman's in that the initiative, the first move, was God's. The idea of building the ark must have been as strange to Noah as it was to everybody else. We wouldn't be surprised if there was just a little bit of worry in Noah's mind that he was going to be locked in the menagerie for a very long summer! But Noah believed that what God said was true, and what God commanded was right. And he obeyed God. His faith was obedience to God.

Faith and Unbelief

One of Jesus' followers, Thomas, is the classic example of the 'doubter'. Let's now look at his story.

TOMMY: Dear readers, I wish it to be known that we are not talking about me.

BOBBY: They know that, Tommy. You are known as Super-Tommy, the living leg-end.

TOMMY: Am I really? Thanks, Bobby.

BOBBY: You're welcome, Tommy. Anyway, let's get back to the other Tommy, the doubting one.

On the evening of that first day of the week, when the disciples were together, with the doors locked for fear of the Jews, Jesus came and stood among them and said, 'Peace be with you!' After he said this, he showed them his hands and side. The disciples were overjoyed when they saw the Lord . . .

Now Thomas (called Didymus), one of the Twelve, was not with the disciples when Jesus came. So the other disciples told him, 'We have seen the Lord!' But he said to them, 'Unless I see the nail marks in his hands and put my finger where the nails were, and put my hand into his side, I will not believe it.'

A week later his disciples were in the house again, and Thomas was with them. Though the doors were locked, Jesus came and stood among them and said, 'Peace be with you!' Then he said to Thomas, 'Put your finger here; see my hands. Reach out your hand and put it into my side. Stop doubting and believe.'

Thomas said to him, 'My Lord and my God!'

Then Jesus told him, 'Because you have seen me, you have believed; blessed are those who have not seen and yet have believed' (John 20:19–29).

Thomas's problem was not doubt in the usual sense. It wasn't that he didn't have enough evidence. It wasn't that he couldn't be sure. It wasn't that he didn't believe in Jesus. It was that he made a deliberate choice not to believe what the others were saying. 'Unless I see,' he said, 'I will not believe.' Now the reason for Thomas's unbelief is clear enough. Imagine all your friends are going out and you can't. When they come back, they've had such a great time, they keep banging on about it. 'You should have been there, it was just so funny! I've never had a night like it!' What would you feel? Most of us would feel bitterly disappointed; most of us would want to think it couldn't have been *that* good. We wouldn't want to believe, because we'd have missed out!

That was Thomas's problem. The thing is, Jesus knew how he was feeling, and knew what he had been saying, and he just showed him. He gave Thomas a greater privilege in some ways than he gave the others, by answering his par ticular difficulties, showing that he valued

Thomas. Thomas couldn't hold on to his resentment a minute longer. He had to confess Jesus as Lord and God. Notice that he says, '*my* Lord and *my* God' – he knew Jesus was Lord and God before, but he thought he'd missed the party. He had faith all along. He just refused to exercise it because of his disappointment.

Different Kinds of Faith, the Same Lord

For the woman Jesus healed, faith was desperate need, and a certainty that Jesus could do something. For Noah, faith was believing what God told him, and obeying. For Thomas, faith was letting go of his resentment and admitting that Jesus is Lord. You can see that in none of these cases was faith a matter of working yourself up into a strange psychic state so that normal rules of living don't apply. You don't have to leave your brain behind when you become a Christian.

You may have some need, as we did, that impels you to turn to God. You may be quietly growing in confidence that the evidence of the world and the Bible points to the fact that God is like we claim he is. Or you may feel that God has let you down in the past, and you've turned away from him. Need, conviction or bitterness, he can deal with it all. You can plead, argue, agree, or complain with God. He can take it! Do it *with* him, and it is an expression of faith.

BOBBY: I was a role model for unbelief. I read all the books on all the religions, but none of them satisfied me. Even the Bible didn't satisfy me, because I didn't have faith. It was only when I desperately needed help that I found I had faith, like the woman we've talked about. Then I really wanted to know God. I really wanted answers. I didn't want to go it alone any more. Nothing else mattered but knowing God and getting forgiveness for my sins.

Not everyone has this experience, but there's always something that drives you on. You can't come to faith by accident. Once you have faith, things change. A butterfly starts its life as a caterpillar, then it builds a cocoon around itself. After a while, it emerges from the cocoon as a beautiful butterfly. It's like that with us. We surround ourselves with possessions, problems and worldly concerns like a cocoon. But by faith in Jesus we can leave our cocoon and start to live life as it should be lived, as God wants us to live!

Repentance

It's a big word for one of the hardest things.
Coming to God is not just about faith, about
wanting a fresh start. It's coming to *God*, and
God is holy and pure. We aren't. This is surely
something that none of us can fool ourselves
about. We know what we've done, what we've
been like, and though we may not like the term
'sinner', that is what we are. We don't mean to
say that everybody has 'lived in sin' in the
modern sense of the words, or everybody is a
liar and a murderer. But everyone has not lived
up to their own ideals, we guess, and certainly
everyone has failed to live in the loving and
obedient way Jesus did. John is very blunt about
this point:

> If we claim to be without sin, we deceive
> ourselves and the truth is not in us. If we
> confess our sins, [God] is faithful and just
> and will forgive us our sins and purify us
> from all unrighteousness. If we claim we
> have not sinned, we make him out to be a
> liar and his word has no place in our lives (1
> John 1:8–10).

Paul says the same thing: 'all have sinned and fall short of the glory of God' (Rom. 3:23). No-one is better than anyone else in this. We all need to repent and be forgiven by God, because all sin is sin against God. If we try and say to him that we're good enough, it's like a man with a penny trying to bribe a millionaire into being his friend because they are alike in being wealthy! Jesus told a story about two people to illustrate this point.

To some who were confident of their own righteousness and looked down on everybody else, Jesus told this parable: 'Two men went up to the temple to pray, one a Pharisee and the other a tax collector. The Pharisee stood up and prayed about himself: "God, I thank you that I am not like all other men – robbers, evildoers, adulterers – or even like this tax collector. I fast twice a week and give a tenth of all I get."

'But the tax collector stood at a distance. He would not even look up to heaven, but beat his breast and said, "God, have mercy on me, a sinner."

'I tell you that this man, rather than the other, went home justified before God. For everyone who exalts himself will be humbled, and he who humbles himself will be exalted' (Luke 18:9–14).

To Jesus' audience, Pharisees were the most religious people known. To carry out all the religious ceremonies correctly, they had to be very serious about what they were doing. But Jesus says it makes no difference if you aren't forgiven by God. It is not what other people think of you, or what you think of other people that makes the important difference, it is whether you are accepted by God. Because he repented and asked for forgiveness, the tax collector (about as popular then as they are now, but much less honest) was accepted by God. The Pharisee got nowhere.

For anyone who can accept the obvious – that we are all in the same boat as far as sin is concerned – and wants to do something about it, the Bible has some very good news. Paul wrote to the Romans, 'God demonstrates his own love for us in this: While we were still sinners, Christ died for us' (Rom. 5:8). And again, 'The wages of sin is death, but the gift of God is eternal life in Christ Jesus our Lord' (Rom. 6:23). Coming to God means asking God for his mercy and forgiveness, and accepting the gift of new life that God gives. This is what being converted means.

Conversion

BOBBY: It's a strange word to use, isn't it,
conversion? It sounds like something you do
with cookers or central heating, to change
them to a different kind of gas.

TOMMY: Listen, stupid!

BOBBY: Don't call me 'listen'!

TOMMY: Conversion is a word used to mean
change or adapt to a new or different purpose.
In other words, to be born again!

BOBBY: Who's a clever little boy, then?

Bobby's picture of a new power source is a good
illustration of what it means to be converted.
Repentance is turning away from our sin and
self-sufficiency, conversion is being plugged in to
God's power for living. Our purpose in life
changes from doing what we want, to doing
what pleases God. The change involved touches
every part of us. Jesus changes us into something
lovely in his eyes, he touches our hearts, souls,
minds and bodies. He changes us to the very
depth of our being.

You might be thinking, 'Yes, this sounds

wonderful, and I want it. But really, I'm not good enough, I've done too many things that are wrong, and got too deep into the mire to get out that easily.' If this is the kind of thing you're thinking, Jesus has a special promise:

> Whoever comes to me I will never drive away. For I have come down from heaven not to do my will but to do the will of him who sent me. And this is the will of him who sent me, that I shall lose none of all that he has given me, but raise them up at the last day. For my Father's will is that everyone who looks to the Son and believes in him shall have eternal life, and I will raise him up at the last day (John 6:37–40).

It is Jesus' power that saves, not our effort. Jesus will raise you up, if you trust him. He will change you. All the awesome power of God will be at work in you. You have Jesus' promise.

So then What?

So where do we go from here? The decision is yours, in one sense at least. We believe that the sensible thing is to ask yourself whether the picture we have described, of ourselves and the situation the world is in, makes sense. Is the Bible fantasy, or is its analysis of us realistic? If the analysis is right, do you want to change, or do you want to carry on as if everything was okay?

We can change, and we've given an outline of the basic steps. The first is faith: a need for change, a conviction that God can help us. The second is repentance: coming to a holy God, and admitting that we've not been the kind of person he created us to be; we've sinned against him and against other people. The third is conversion: asking Jesus to come into our life and change it, to take away the sin and guilt, and replace it with his love and power for living his way. If we do this, Jesus says we will be born again, and be given new life. It's both very simple and very hard. Simple, because there's no complicated set of rituals; hard, because we're handing over our lives to God and no longer relying on ourselves.

You can do this at your own pace, in your own way. Take time over it, because it's a big decision. Tell God about the things you worry about, or the things that you're unsure of. If you have a Christian friend you trust, ask them to pray with you. If you have never prayed before, and don't know where to start, here's a simple prayer you could use:

> God, I come to you as a sinner, and I know you are holy. I also know that you love me, despite what I am. I believe that Jesus died so that my sins could be forgiven and dealt with. So I ask you to forgive me, and give me a new life and a fresh start. I want Jesus to be Lord of my life, so give me the power to live for him. I'm relying on you, Lord, to change me. I believe you have heard my prayer and are living in me right now. Thank you for your love.

What Happens?

TOMMY: When I first asked the Lord into my life, I felt different, but not as though I had changed completely. It was only in my bedroom that I really confessed my sin to him, and asked Jesus to be my saviour. It was then that I knew he was really with me, and that I was really forgiven.

BOBBY: My experience was totally the opposite of Tommy's. I knew instantly! The minute I asked the Lord into my life, everything changed.

The main change at this stage is your standing before God. You become a saint! This is the Bible's word for someone who is a Christian. If you've ever said, 'I'm no saint', you'll have to take it back! It doesn't mean that you suddenly become all pious, it means that God accepts you and forgives you. You become like a new person. It might be an earth-shattering experience or it might not. If you confess sins and hurts that you have bottled up for ages, you might cry as God cleans them out. If you're the sort of person who is always trying, driven by your ambition or will, you might experience a quietness and peace. If you have come to believe after turning your back on God and religion, you might simply feel as if you've come home. You may feel no different at all, but how you feel is not the most important thing. What has happened is the most important: there is a new you!

Welcome!

Every true Christian is now your brother or sister. Together, we make up the body of Christ, the church, and God has given us each other as an encouragement and a help. The Holy Spirit lives in each one of us, and works through the church especially to bring about an environment of love in which we can grow to be more like Jesus. Welcome to the body of Christ!

Chapter 6

Growing as a Christian

Seed and Fruit

When you become a Christian, all kinds of things change. It's a new start, a new way of living. This means two things. First, it's different from what went before. Second, it's something that develops and grows. If you think of a seed, you wouldn't be that pleased if, a year after you planted it, you just dug it up and found it exactly as it was before. You'd want it to change – to become a flower, or to change into a carrot; and you'd want it to develop, not just pop out of its shell and do nothing. Or if you had a fruit bush, you'd expect, given the right conditions, for the bush to grow and produce fruit. The growth and fruit depend on the kind of seed or shrub, and the way the seed or shrub is tended and cultivated.

It's the same with the Christian life. There's a radical change, and it results in growth and fruit. This is what Jesus taught his followers:

I am the true vine and my Father is the gardener ... Remain in me, and I will remain in you. No branch can bear fruit by itself; it must remain in the vine. Neither can you bear fruit unless you remain in me.

I am the vine; you are the branches. If a man remains in me and I in him, he will bear much fruit; apart from me you can do nothing. If anyone does not remain in me, he is like a branch that is thrown away and withers; such branches are picked up, thrown into the fire and burned. If you remain in me and my words remain in you, ask whatever you wish, and it will be given you. This is to my Father's glory, that you bear much fruit, showing yourselves to be my disciples (John 15:1–8).

The point of this image is that Christians become part of the vine that is Jesus himself. The fruit is the kind of 'fruit' Jesus himself grew: love, goodness, patience, purity, selflessness, and so on. But we can't do it on our own. He gives us the nourishment and goodness, like a tree's roots and trunk feed nourishment to the branches. At the same time, we have to do our part, what Jesus calls remaining in him and letting his words remain in us. So how do we do our part? Three basic things are: praying; reading the Bible, God's word; and joining a church.

Prayer

Prayer is the normal way we talk with God. It is the language of faith, and like any language, you can get by in it quite quickly, but it takes a good while to get to be fluent. It is communication with God, not just us talking. God speaks to us, guides us, encourages and strengthens us through prayer.

Jesus was a man of prayer. He spent a lot of time with his Father in prayer. In the Gospels we learn that he used to get up early, go off on his own, and pray. He prayed long and hard before big decisions like who to choose as his followers. He prayed especially before the ordeal of his death, and we know he asked his Father to forgive those who tortured him on the cross itself. You might say, 'But if Jesus was the Son of God, why did he need to pray?' Well, he needed to pray for the same reason that we

need to talk to and respond to friends or spouses.
If you don't speak to your husband because you
just know that you are married, the marriage
might soon be in trouble! Talking is a way of
building and sustaining a relationship. Prayer is
just the same. Jesus needed it and so do we.

How To Pray

Jesus taught his followers to pray simply, hon-
estly and in faith.

> When you pray, go into your room, close the
> door and pray to your Father, who is unseen.
> Then your Father, who sees what is done in
> secret, will reward you. And when you pray,
> do not keep on babbling like pagans, for they
> think they will be heard because of their
> many words. Do not be like them, for your
> Father knows what you need before you ask
> him (Matt. 6:6–8).

Then he gives them the model prayer, which is
used the world over, the Lord's Prayer.

> Our Father in heaven, hallowed be your
> name, your kingdom come, your will be

done on earth as it is in heaven. Give us
today our daily bread. Forgive us our debts,
as we also have forgiven our debtors. And
lead us not into temptation, but deliver us
from the evil one.

For if you forgive men when they sin
against you, your heavenly Father will also
forgive you. But if you do not forgive men
their sins, your Father will not forgive your
sins (Matt. 6:9–15).

When we're praying, we're not trying to impress
God or anybody else. It doesn't matter very
much whether we say things aloud or in our
heads, whether we use spiritual language or
everyday language, whether we repeat ourselves, or stumble over words, or lose track,
or our minds wander occasionally. Our Father
knows what we're like, he just wants to hear us
and be with us. It's best to keep it simple and
straightforward. Tell God you love him, and
thank him for the things he's done for you.
Ask him to forgive you for the things you've
done or said that you know were wrong, and for
the things that you should have done but didn't
do. Talk to him about the things that you've got
to do, things that are bugging you, things that
are difficult. Ask him for the things you need.

Try to give time to quiet thought, when you are not actually asking for anything, but allowing God to communicate his love to you. Finally, thank him for being with you, and see if you can hold on to his love and peace as you go on to do other things. Remember you can carry on praying even when you are doing other things.

Prayer is an effective and powerful weapon against evil. We have to learn to use it wisely. Peter was locked in prison and chained to two soldiers for preaching, and the Christians were praying for him. God sent an angel who released Peter and led him out of the prison. So Peter went to where the church people were praying, and they were so amazed that they didn't even let him in for a while because they could hardly believe it! (Acts 12:4–17) On another occasion Paul and Silas were also in prison for preaching, and they were praying and singing God's praises, when an earthquake freed them from their chains. They didn't run away, but stayed to tell the jailer how he could be saved. He and all his family believed (Acts 16:22–34). God has no favourites, and we are little different from Peter, Paul or Silas. Our prayers, by God's grace, can change things.

These stories show that God does wonderful things in answer to prayer. But the Christians who were praying for Peter didn't quite expect the answer they got from God. God wants us to have faith and pray 'big' prayers, but he also wants us to be honest. That means, for most of us, starting with the things we believe God can change – perhaps things in our own lives, or tricky situations we face. Our faith will grow as we see how God helps us through these things. There may be disappointments, too, which we'll need to ask God to help us deal with. We mustn't pretend that everything is easy and simple once we're Christians. As our faith grows, we can pray more widely, and hear God's promptings more readily, and so pray more dramatic and effective prayers.

Just one more thing before we leave this subject for a while. Sometimes you may find that you feel as if your prayers are bouncing off the ceiling, or that you're just talking to yourself. It may be difficult to find time or to concentrate. You may feel as if you've got nothing to say. These things sometimes happen. Different people deal with these situations differently. Some people can talk them through with God. Some people find help by using books of prayers. Others may want to read a book about prayer. Still others may get together with another Christian to pray. But the important thing is to keep time for God in our lives. God can fill emptiness, he doesn't usually stop overbusyness!

BOBBY: Tommy! I can feel a joke coming on!

TOMMY: Oh, no! Just when the book was getting interesting.

BOBBY: It's another one about the Bible. Who's the smallest man in the Bible?

TOMMY: I don't know, who is the smallest man in the Bible?

BOBBY: Bildad the Shuhite! He's in the book of Job. (Shoe-height, get it?)

TOMMY: Okay, let's get on with the book. Prayer, to get back to the subject, has helped me all my Christian life. Whatever happens, good or bad, I pray to God about it, giving him thanks and praise. As Christians we depend on God totally, and that's something that only comes through prayer.

BOBBY: My friend and pastor gave me a good idea that works wonders in my life. He said that when you go to bed at night, if you pray until you go to sleep, your mind is focused on Jesus, and when you wake up you may find you are still focused on him. If then you start the new day by praying as soon as you wake up, it can help your whole day to centre on Jesus. That's a step towards 'praying without ceasing' which Paul tells his Christian friends to do. Prayer is so heart-lifting. It's wonderful to know that God cares enough to listen to what we say.

TOMMY: I keep praying for Bobby to get funnier, but I can't be praying hard enough!

BOBBY: That's funny, Tommy. There are lots of people wishing I was funnier.

Don't worry about prayer. It isn't always easy, and you have to find your own way of doing it. Certainly you have to work out how to fit it into your programme as a deliberate act of obedience to God. But if you can stick with it, God promises you his peace:

Do not be anxious about anything, but in everything, by prayer and petition, with thanksgiving, present your requests to God. And the peace of God, which transcends all understanding, will guard your hearts and minds in Christ Jesus (Phil. 4:6–7).

Reading the Bible

God speaks through the Bible. This is why we call it God's word. When you start to read it on a regular basis, and get to know what it says, it becomes a kind of friend. It helps you to know what pleases God, it helps you to praise him, it helps you to understand what is happening in the world, it brings comfort when you are suffering. We believe the Bible is a true record of God's dealings with Israel and with Christians. Paul wrote to his friend Timothy about the Bible in this way:

> All Scripture is God-breathed and is useful for teaching, rebuking, correcting and train-ing in righteousness, so that the man of God may be thoroughly equipped for every good work (2 Tim. 3:16–17).

The word 'God-breathed' is sometimes trans-lated 'inspired by God'. What Paul is saying here is that the source of the Bible is God. The Holy Spirit is God's 'breath', so the Holy Spirit is especially involved first in the writing of the Bible, and then in our reading of it. God trains us through the Bible, by telling us what kind of things we should and should not be doing. By understanding the Bible and taking its message to heart, we get the equipment we need to live as Christians.

But as we said before, the Bible isn't the easiest book in the world to understand. It's important that you get hold of a Bible that speaks your kind of language. If you go to a Christian bookshop they will be able to show you the range of Bible translations available, and recommend one for you. Or you could try reading the same passage in several different versions and see which one you find easiest to follow. Some Bibles have notes at the back or on the same page which tell you what the passage means. There are also lots of Bible-reading notes and plans. Again, it's best to start with something designed for beginners, but then you can try different ways of reading and different styles of notes. Above all, we need to keep at it when it comes to reading the Bible. Try reading and discussing it with someone who has been a Christian longer than you, or if there's something you don't understand, ask your minister or pastor about it.

BOBBY: I've got a study Bible that explains to me the passages I'm reading. It's not that I'm thick, but I do find the Bible heavy going, without someone or something to explain it.

TOMMY: I must have been one of the best at asking questions! Before I became a Christian, Bobby bought me a Bible for Christmas. Well, I started to look at this Bible, trying to find questions I thought I could catch Bobby out with. So I would ask him these questions and he would eventually answer them. A few years later, I became a Christian too, and I carried on reading the Bible, but now I found deeper questions, and things I didn't understand, but genuinely wanted to know about. So while were driving somewhere in the car, I would ask Bobby these questions. 'Hmm,' he would say, 'That's a good one. I'll tell you tomorrow.' Sure enough, the next day he would give me an answer to the questions. I started thinking to myself that Bobby was indeed very knowledgeable about the Bible, and possibly a theological genius! It wasn't until a few years later that I found out that when I asked him questions, he rang round all his friends to find out the answers! So you see, if you don't ask, you don't find out!

Possible Problems

Because the Bible can be difficult, some people don't read it regularly or even at all. With most books you start at the beginning and read through to the end, but if you try that with the Bible, you may come unstuck! Leviticus and Deuteronomy are not entertaining books. Important, but not entertaining. As we said earlier, the New Testament is easier for beginners to read, and we all need to know as much of Jesus' teaching by heart as possible. That way, it becomes part of you, and it strengthens you in times of decision or difficulty.

Some Christians don't read the Bible very much because they've got hung up on one or two difficulties that they don't know the answer to. God speaks through the whole of the Bible, and by consistent reading, we get to know the kind of things that please him. If there are things that trouble you, and you can't get an answer straight away, put them on the back burner. File them in the back of your mind and, in the middle of the night sometime, you'll wake up with an explanation! Or the matter will come up in discussion, or in a sermon, and you'll understand. But the important thing to remember is that there is plenty in the Bible that is easy to understand, and is useful in our Christian lives. We shouldn't miss that because there are things we don't understand. We have to remember that the Bible is two thousand and more years old.

Some Helpful Tips

Here are some things that we've found useful as we read the Bible:

1. The Bible is God's word, as we've said. The Holy Spirit lives in you if you are a Christian. Ask him to help you as you read the Bible. Ask him to speak to you in your heart and mind as you read.

2. Particularly in the stories you find in the Bible, use your imagination. Try to imagine what it might have felt like to be Joseph when his brothers sold him as a slave, or what it felt like to be the prodigal son, wanting to eat the pig food because he was so hungry.

3. If something strikes you as being a special message for you, or a lesson that you want to learn, or if it tells

you something new or special about God, then underline it or highlight it in your Bible. You can also write down the reference in a notebook, and possibly write with it what you thought at the time.

4. Try to memorise some of the passages you highlight. Most of the quotes from the Bible we have used in this book have been passages we've jotted down in our notebooks and tried to learn. These passages become like landmarks in our Christian lives, and they can help us see how we are growing in knowledge of God.

Finding a Church

Being a Christian is about growing spiritually, and as well as prayer and the Bible, God gives us other Christians to help us. When we share together with other Christians the things that matter to us in our relationship with God, it's what is called fellowship. Fellowship is all about being Christians together: praising God together, learning together, praying together; sharing each other's sufferings and joys, joining with others to tell our neighbours about Jesus. All these things are part of what being the church is.

What's Special about the Church?

Jesus attended the Jewish equivalent of church, the synagogue, regularly. He learned the Scriptures as a child and young man at the synagogue, and when he started his special ministry, he taught in the synagogue. So he thought learning with others was important. But more than that, he told his followers that he would be with them in a powerful way when they were together: 'If two of you on earth agree about anything you ask for, it will be done for you by my Father in heaven. For where two or three come together in my name, there am I with them' (Matt. 18:19–20).

Worship, prayer and fellowship all centre on Jesus. We either do it all in his name, focusing on him, or we're wasting our time. Jesus is amongst us when we are together as Christians because the church is the body of Christ. Even two or three people in someone's front room can be the church where Jesus is present.

What this means is that a church is not a building! A church is Christian people meeting together, and finding that Jesus is with them.

We're almost programmed to think of the church as a building surrounded by graves, visited once a week by people in their best clothes, but rather eerie for the rest of the week. Perhaps that's why people don't want to be part of the church! But the building is just a building. Churches meet in terraced houses, in cinemas, in schools, in pub rooms *and* of course in the buildings we call churches. The building is not that important. It's what goes on in it, and amongst the people, that matters.

What Does the Church Do?

When Jesus had gone up to heaven, his followers continued to meet to pray and share together. Luke shows us what the earliest church was like:

> They devoted themselves to the apostles' teaching and to the fellowship, to the breaking of bread and to prayer. Everyone was filled with awe, and many wonders and miraculous signs were done by the apostles. All the believers were together and had everything in common. Selling their possessions and goods, they gave to anyone as he had need. Every day they continued to

meet together in the temple courts. They broke bread in their homes and ate together with glad and sincere hearts, praising God and enjoying the favour of all the people. And the Lord added to their number daily those who were being saved (Acts 2:42–7).

There are lots of 'togethers' in this passage. One of the things the church does is to bring very different people together, and make them into a unit, a body that works together to bring glory to God. Don't expect to find a church where everyone is like you! But when the church is together, there are certain things that we can expect to find, as they were found in this earliest church in the book of Acts: teaching, fellowship, prayer, signs of God's power, sharing, praise and people becoming Christians.

Teaching is done especially in sermons, but also in Bible study and all kinds of other meetings. It's important that the teaching is based on the Bible, is interesting and applies to real life. As Christians we need help to meet the challenges of our society, and clear, relevant teaching from God's word can give us that help. Fellowship can take all sorts of forms, from social events to visiting the sick. It's important that we know each other in the church, and that we love each other with the love of Jesus. Praying together can happen in small groups of two or three, or the church may meet to pray all together. When we pray, we believe that Jesus will do as he promised and give us what we ask for. So we may pray for healing or guidance, or for God's power to change particular situations. It doesn't always happen instantly, but Jesus leads our prayers and guides our thoughts so that we pray for his will.

One of the marks of the early church was the care they showed for those who were disadvantaged. Those who were rich gave to those who were poor. Though it takes different forms, this should still be a mark of the church. We care for those who are sick, we share our possessions so that the needs of all are met. Often this goes on in a very quiet way, so that you wouldn't notice it just by coming into a meeting of the church. We aim to share our possessions and gifts not only with those in our part of the church, but also with Christians in need in other lands, supporting missionaries and mission aid causes, too.

These things we've mentioned naturally lead into joyous worship. We don't know whether the early church sang or chanted or recited or shouted, but we do know they praised God! The style of a church's worship often depends on its history (the tradition it has built up over the years) and its current resources (guitars and organ depend on guitarists and organist!), but the worship should be from the heart. And finally, we don't want to keep the good news of Jesus to ourselves, we want others to know and share the good things God has given us. Our church should encourage us to do this personally, and it should intend to do it as a body. This was Jesus' last command to his followers, 'Go and make disciples of all nations', and with it the promise of his presence, 'and surely I will be with you always' (Matt. 28:19–20).

What's Right for You?

There's a lot about finding a church that is personal. Style of music, number of people, kind of preaching, and so on. Look, though, for most of these marks that we've mentioned. Don't expect to be able to know whether a church is for you straight away. Try to get involved, and get to know people. Look for chances to give time, use your gifts, and share your resources with the people there. Fellow Christians are your family, sharing the same heavenly Father: let them share with you what they have experienced of God and encourage you in your spiritual growth. The early Jewish church suffered a lot, and people were tempted to drift away from the church, but a wise counsellor wrote to them: 'Let us consider how we may spur one another on towards love and good deeds. Let us not give up meeting together, as some are in the habit of doing, but let us encourage one another' (Heb. 10:24–5). See again how much being a Christian is about being involved with other Christians. Someone once said there's no such thing as a 'desert island disc-iple'!

BOBBY: I've been a Christian for a long time, and it's only in the last couple of years that I've felt at home in a church, a church that I can call mine. I tried lots, small and big, but I didn't feel right in any of them. But I knew I had to find one; I knew I had to find a spiritual home where I could pray and worship with others. When I didn't find a church for such a long time, I began to feel a little bit lost. There's a great Gothic church building at the bottom of my road and I saw people going there and I thought for the thousandth time, 'Well, I'll go there and try it.' So I did. One Sunday morning I went down for the service.

As usual, I was running a bit late, so when I arrived the service had already begun. I sneaked in, but surprisingly people smiled at me. I hadn't really experienced this before. People don't like you being late. I thought that when they frowned, it meant you weren't supposed to be enjoying the service!

TOMMY: Just get on with the story, Bobby, and less of the gags.

BOBBY: Where was I? Oh, yes. The minister of this church seemed a nice chap, but he didn't look the sort of man who was going to turn the world upside-down. So although I went back once or twice, I drifted on. Some time later, I saw some people building another church a bit further up the road. This interested me: perhaps this would be the church for me? Once when I was driving by, I stopped and knocked on the main door. It wasn't even finished and opened yet, but a man called John came to the door and showed me round. It was very simple, and he told me a little bit about the history of the church in the area. Then he told me that the minister of the big Gothic church down the road was going to be the minister here.

I was working away for some time, so I

didn't get to the opening of the new building, but when I did go, everybody was so welcoming. The service was simple, and it was all very nice, but it still didn't grab me! But every time I drove past, I felt the Lord telling me to go back there. I ignored him for a while, but he kept telling me. So I went back eventually, and I got to know the minister. I found out that he is a very humble man, but a man who is being used by God in wonderful ways. I found out that he is a real worker for God, spiritually alive, and leading a growing church. I didn't see all this earlier, because I was concentrating on my own ideas about what I wanted. Now I am fully settled in the church, and being part of it, sharing with my brothers and sisters, is one of the best things that has happened to me. The minister is not only a pastor, he is a friend. Our church involves everyone in the services, and we all minister to each other. We are a joyful church, even when there is suffering among us. When we pray together, we have seen the Holy Spirit do miracles.

Now the thing to notice about this is that if I'd stuck with my ideas and not listened to the Lord, I'd have missed all the blessings that God has given me through my church, and I'd probably still be looking!

The Bible tells us we should meet together for our own good. We won't usually find a church that meets every one of our standards or ideas. But in the church there has to be give and take. Some things God will change, some things you can change, and some things you have to live with! But all these things can be part of our spiritual growth!

Chapter 7

Spiritual Warfare

Enemies!

Being a Christian isn't easy. Well, Jesus never
said it would be. And although there are lots of
really good things about being a Christian, you'll
discover very quickly that you have enemies.
Traditionally, these enemies are called the
world, the flesh and the devil. As Christians,
we have to struggle daily against temptations
and wrong thoughts, and against the malice of
the devil. But we have the resources because God
is with us.

The World

Basically, the English-speaking world, the world
we live and work in, runs as though God does

not exist. Many people might say they believe in
God, but they don't want him to influence their
lives. People don't like it if you have higher
moral standards, and they think you're being
superior. Christians get ridiculed and laughed at
because of their beliefs. People think that Christians hide away from reality in their churches,
or need their beliefs because they can't hack it in
the world. For many, Christianity is a wimpish
thing, or is mumbo-jumbo, or a kind of super-
stition: it has nothing to do with work, econom-
ics, science or politics. It gives people a quiet
glow, and is pie in the sky when you die if you
try. These attitudes are typical of what the Bible
refers to as 'the world'.

Just from reading this book, you will know
that none of these attitudes are true to the facts.
Christians face the truth about themselves and
the world more than most. Christians struggle
more with raw reality because so much of it goes
against what we believe is God's will. Christianity has everything to do with work, politics and
the rest. And it's as much about the 'here and
now' as about the 'there and then'! But Jesus
actually promised his followers that there would
be trouble for us: 'In this world you will have
trouble. But take heart! I have overcome the
world' (John 16:33). This comes at the end of

a long passage where Jesus is teaching his
followers what to do and expect as Christians.
What he tells them is simple:

> This is my command: Love each other.
> If the world hates you, keep in mind that it
> hated me first. If you belonged to the world,
> it would love you as its own. As it is, you do
> not belong to the world, but I have chosen
> you out of the world. That is why the world
> hates you . . . If they persecuted me, they
> will persecute you also. If they obeyed my
> teaching, they will obey yours also. They
> will treat you this way because of my name,
> for they do not know the One who sent me
> (John 15:17–21).

This gives the love we have for each other
within the church a very practical purpose.
When we face hostility from the world, we
need the love and acceptance of our brothers
and sisters. As Jesus' servants we can expect
treatment like he received. Christians are per-
secuted in various ways all over the world. In
many countries, their sufferings are very great.
The things we have to bear can be difficult and
depressing, but we probably won't be impris-
oned. However, we can expect rejection and

indifference without doing anything in particular to deserve it.

BOBBY:　An old friend I have known for many years came to visit me the other day. After a while the atmosphere became a bit strained. He was quiet for a moment, and then he said, 'You're not the same since you became a born again Christian.' He thought I would be upset and that I would want to be my old self again. In a way he was right and in a way he was wrong. He was right about me not being the same. God has made me new, and given me peace that I never had before. But he was wrong about me wanting to be my old self. God has given me a better life, and I wouldn't have the old one back if you paid me! I was upset that he saw it that way, though.

TOMMY:　That's a relief. I thought you were going to tell another joke then.

BOBBY:　Don't worry, Tommy, I've got one ready for the end of the book.

TOMMY:　Somehow I thought you would have.

The world, in this special sense that it has very often in the Bible, is everything that is ungodly, against God's rule or simply not bothered about God. And it acts on us to wear down our faith and belittle it. Conquering the world is about holding on to Jesus and our faith. John says this:

> This is love for God: to obey his commands. And his commands are not burdensome, for everyone born of God has overcome the world. This is the victory that has overcome the world, even our faith. Who is it that overcomes the world? Only he who believes that Jesus is the Son of God (1 John 5:3–5).

That's why we need prayer and Bible reading, fellowship and encouragement. These are our weapons against the enemy which is the world.

The Flesh

We all have desires, appetites and needs which are part of our bodily make-up. The kind of things we do, the things we think about, the ideals we set ourselves, reflect the choices we make about which desires and needs are most important. This sounds heavy, but what we're saying is that 'the flesh' involves more than sex! Our nature is basically selfish and sinful, and as such it draws us away from God. That's why we need a new nature and a new life, given to us by God. In older translations of the Bible, the words 'sinful nature' are 'the flesh' in this passage from Paul:

> Those who live according to the sinful nature have their minds set on what that nature desires; but those who live in accordance with the Spirit have their minds set on what the Spirit desires. The mind of the sinful man is death, but the mind controlled by the Spirit is life and peace, because the sinful mind is hostile to God. It does not submit to God's law, nor can it do so. Those controlled by the sinful nature cannot please God (Rom. 8:5–8).

There are two alternatives: we can live controlled by our desires and appetites, or we can live controlled by the Holy Spirit. Because they become part of our personality, our habits and desires do actually control us. There must be times when we all wished we'd not done something, but couldn't stop ourselves. Anger, greed, lust, pride, are things that take over and deform our personalities. That's why, when we repent, God promises to forget our sins. Jeremiah prophesied about the new covenant God was going to make, way back before Jesus' time, and God says, 'I will forgive their wickedness and will remember their sins no more' (Jer. 31:34). When God forgets, as only God can forget, he forgets absolutely. This means that it is as if we had never done or thought or said those things that we have repented of. So we can be free of them. They don't have to control us any more. God won't bring them up again, so we don't have to either.

Having said that, old habits die hard. Some things hit you again and again. The only thing to do when the temptation comes is to pray. And if you fall into sin, come back to God and ask for forgiveness. None of us is perfect, but all of us can live a life controlled by the Holy Spirit. We do this by forming new habits to replace the old ones. Prayer and Bible study are obvious ones, but there are many other things that can develop our skills, engage our minds, and help us to grow more like Jesus. Paul advises Christians,

Whatever is true, whatever is noble, whatever is right, whatever is pure, whatever is lovely, whatever is admirable – if anything is excellent or praiseworthy – think about such things. Whatever you have learned or received or heard from me, or seen in me – put it into practice. And the God of peace will be with you (Phil. 4:8–9).

There's no big secret about living a holy life. It's tough, admittedly, but it's simple: fill your mind with the things of God, good and wholesome things, and do what God tells you! That's how we conquer the enemy of 'the flesh'.

The Devil

You may think that no-one takes the devil seriously, all that stuff about horns and spiky tail. Well, we don't believe in the horns and all that, but the Bible is very clear that our main enemy is the devil. 'Satan' in Hebrew means one who accuses. In the book of Revelation, the devil is a serpent, a dragon, the one who leads the world astray (Rev. 12:9–13). He is thrown out of heaven, and tries to set up a kingdom on earth. In 1 Peter 5:8 he is called a roaring lion, looking for people to devour. These are pictures of the devil's nature: savage, hateful, opposing God and goodness, deceitful, lying, and within limits, powerful.

The one thing he isn't, though, is equal with God. Though he can attack God's people, and wound us; though he can tempt us and accuse us and try to persuade us that God can't love us, he has no ultimate power over us. Once we belong to Jesus, nothing can snatch us out of his hand (John 10:28). Films like *The Exorcist* try to show the devil as incredibly powerful. In these films, people have to do all kinds of things to defeat him. But in reality, he has no power over God's people. James puts the matter very simply: 'Submit yourselves . . . to God. Resist the devil, and he will flee from you. Come near to God and he will come near to you. Wash your hands, you sinners, and purify your hearts, you double-minded' (Jas. 4:7–8).

The devil can only get a hold over us through sin. We entertain the devil when we persist in sin. But if we resist him, by always turning to the Lord for forgiveness and strength, he will run a mile! If you think about it, the devil will try all the devious tricks in the book to tempt us and turn us away from God. If every time we feel the temptation, we pray to God, the devil will give up eventually because he's only making us more prayerful. It may take time, and we may weaken, but we will overcome him by God's power in the end.

We've also got armour to wear to protect us from attack:

Be strong in the Lord and in his mighty power. Put on the full armour of God so that you can take your stand against the devil's schemes. For our struggle is not against flesh and blood, but against the rulers, against the authorities, against the powers of this dark world and against the spiritual forces of evil in the heavenly realms. Therefore put on the full armour of God, so that when the day of evil comes, you may be able to stand your ground, and after you have done everything, to stand. Stand firm then, with the belt of truth buckled around your waist, with the breastplate of right-eousness in place, and with your feet fitted with the readiness that comes from the gospel of peace. In addition to all this, take up the shield of faith, with which you can extinguish all the flaming arrows of the evil one. Take the helmet of salvation and the sword of the Spirit, which is the word of God. And pray in the Spirit on all occasions with all kinds of prayers and requests. With this in mind, be alert and always keep on praying for all the saints (Eph. 6:10–18).

The picture of the armour here is taken from the Roman soldier's equipment. It may seem a bit complex, but it isn't really. Paul urges us to protect ourselves by surrounding ourselves with the truth: the truth about ourselves and the truth about God. We should protect our hearts by imitating the righteousness of Jesus. Being ready to share the gospel protects us from walking into temptation. Our faith can block everything the devil tempts us with, because we know that the ultimate victory belongs to Jesus. We protect our minds with the assurance that we are saved by God's grace, not because of what we have done. And we use God's word to fight and advance against the enemy. All this is backed up by constant prayer, for ourselves and for others in the battle.

This is a very encouraging passage. These things that make up the armour of God are not strange and difficult things. They are all the things that being a Christian is about. What Paul is saying is, 'Practise your Christianity, and you will defeat the devil.' Another thing to notice is that Paul doesn't expect us to crush evil empires and conquer everything that is against God: the victory is ours if in the end we stand, firm in our faith. That result might take in quite a bit of falling on the way, but we can do it with God's armour and the Spirit's power.

BOBBY: Anyway, folks, happy battles!

TOMMY: Bobby!

BOBBY: I'm only joking, Tommy. And that reminds me, I think it's about time for another joke.

TOMMY: I wish I hadn't said anything!

BOBBY: The devil came to St Peter one day and challenged heaven to a game of football, and St Peter said, 'How can you win, Satan? All the famous footballers are up here.' 'How can I lose?' answered Satan. 'All the referees are down here!'

TOMMY: But referees are sometimes quite nice people!

BOBBY: It's a joke, Tommy!

TOMMY: I know. But Bobby has made a serious point. We have to laugh at the devil, because he's weak and pathetic. He can't touch us if we stay close to God.

We aren't alone in spiritual warfare: every Christian faces it, and that's why it's important to stay close to God and stay close to your church. As we face these attacks together and pray, the devil will run away like the coward he is.

Living for God

There are always two sides to living as a Christian. You might call them being and doing, or status and practice, or even holiness and usefulness! Basically it's about what God has done for us, and how we respond. God has made us new, we have to get on and live the new life. God has cleaned us up from our sin, now we have to live lives that please him. God has made us brothers and sisters of Jesus, we have to grow in the family likeness.

It's very tempting simply to enjoy the peace and wonder of being a Christian when you first come to God. There are so many things to discover and so much to enjoy. We can become like little children given the run of a sweetshop. But we have to remember that the sweets are for sharing and also to give us energy to go out and live powerful lives. Jesus' teachings were meant to be put into action.

Holiness and Usefulness

God is holy. By Jesus' death, he took away our sins, so that we can be holy. 'Holy' means different, set apart for some special purpose. So in the Bible it tells us that God is different from us in his total purity and goodness, but that he makes it possible for us to be like him. We don't become holy by going to church or being kind to people. We are given holiness by God. It's like new clothes: we are given holiness, but we have to grow into it.

All kinds of things might come into your mind when you think of holiness – being poor, wearing a monk's habit, walking around with hands together and eyes closed, chanting hymns. But actually holiness is a very practical way of life, and when it's lived out, it becomes usefulness.

BOBBY: Before I was a Christian I was frightened that I wouldn't match up to what Jesus wanted of me. I thought I couldn't let go of my lust, drinking and violence, and become 'holy'. But I was wrong. When I stopped worrying about what I could do, and just let Jesus give me what I needed, my life changed. And believe me, I am not a monk!

TOMMY: You're not far off.

BOBBY: What do you mean by that?

TOMMY: Let's put it this way, you have a tendency to live frugally.

BOBBY: Are you saying I'm tight with my money?

TOMMY: Tight! Bobby's the only man I know who can peel and orange in his pocket! With a knife!

BOBBY: Folks, Tommy told that joke last night and three empty seats walked out!

Holiness means having new values; trying to see things as God sees them; loving; caring; forgiving; telling the truth; giving our best at work; going out of our way to help others. If this sounds hard, think for a minute of the alternative. Sin may have attractions, but it leaves bitterness and sadness behind; it hurts people and damages relationships. So holiness takes effort, but it doesn't take away your zest for life or enjoyment of happiness, it actually increases them! Paul wrote this:

I urge you, brothers, in view of God's mercy, to offer your bodies as living sacrifices, holy and pleasing to God – which is your spiritual worship. Do not conform any longer to the pattern of this world, but be transformed by the renewing of your mind. Then you will be able to test and approve what God's will is –

his good, pleasing and perfect will (Rom.
12:1–2).

Paul goes on to give details of what he means by
this. It's about being humble, getting on with
other Christians, serving, doing tasks in the
church, and above all, loving others. But doing
things as living sacrifices is spiritual worship! So
holiness is practical, and practicality can be
worship. That's something to think about.

Depending on God

We believe there are two kinds of Christians.
There are part-time Christians and there are full-
time Christians. If you just go to church on a
Sunday and leave it at that, and God doesn't
enter your thoughts for the rest of the week, then
you are a part-time Christian. This may sound
harsh, but you're not giving God what he
deserves. You're not putting him first in your
life. We all need to take a good hard look at our
lives to see that God comes first, before work,
money, and even family. Jesus gave up everything, down to his own life, to save us: we can't
respond with less than everything. Paul put it this
way: 'You are not your own; you were bought at

a price. Therefore honour God with your body'
(1 Cor. 6:19–20). Paul is talking particularly
about sexual morality at this point, but the
principle applies much more widely. What we
do shows who or what we serve. If we only do
what we want, and what we feel like doing,
we're not serving God. Everything we do should
show that God is first in our lives, because Jesus
bought us back from sin and death. We are his,
and we need to depend on him.

BOBBY: I have been a Christian for ten years,
but it's only in about the last three years that
I've allowed God to control my life. Don't get
me wrong, I loved and worshipped God, and I
told other people about him. But I didn't allow
him full control of my life. He had about 75 per
cent, but I kept back the other 25 per cent. At
the same time, I used to wonder why I wasn't
growing as a Christian. Now I know. It's a
learning process, but it's something we should
all learn, sooner rather than later.

God knows what we need. He also knows what
is good for us. Sometimes there is a conflict
between what we want and what God wants.
But he's our Father, and like a father, he gently
persuades us and helps us to accept his purpose.

We might be like little children and cry, kick and scream, but he can handle that. He knows it's better for us to complain to him than for us to go away and do our own thing. There are some real struggles for most of us, especially early on in our Christian lives. But the more we learn of God, the more we depend on him, and the more we trust ourselves to his way. When we look back, we will see that he has done everything for our good. An unknown soldier wrote this:

I asked God for strength that I might achieve.
I was made weak so that I might learn humbly to obey.

I asked God for health that I might do greater things.
I was given infirmity that I might do better things.

I asked for riches that I might be happy.
I was given poverty that I might be wise.

I asked for power that I might have the praise of men.
I was given weakness that I might feel the need for God.

I asked for all things that I might enjoy life.
I was given life that I might enjoy all things.

I got nothing that I asked for,
But everything that I hoped for.
Almost despite myself, my unspoken prayers
    were answered.
I am amongst all men most richly blessed.

That says it all. When we give ourselves totally
to God, he works for our good and his glory
through our lives. When his Spirit is at work in
us, he uses us in special ways. He may use us to
heal people, he may give us his words for
building up the church, he may give us gifts of
leadership, or gifts of service. There are many
things that he wants to give us so that we can do
his will. We will close this chapter with a very
simple poem called 'Give Me':

Give me work to do,
Give me health,
Give me joy in simple things,
Give me an eye for beauty,

A tongue for truth,
A heart that loves,
A mind that reasons,
A sympathy that understands.

Give me neither malice nor envy,
But a true kindness,
And a noble common sense.

At the end of each day
Give me a book
And a friend with whom I can be silent.

S. M. Frazier

Epilogue

What Christianity Means to Us

TOMMY: Christianity to me means a new way of life. It's an exciting life knowing that there is someone I can rely on, someone who never sleeps, someone who is always there when I need him. And I need him all the time, believe me! As Bobby and I sing in our gospel shows, 'He's the rock that doesn't roll.'

Jesus means everything to my family and me. He has given me a whole new outlook on life. Everything changed when I became a Christian, but then it had to. He not only came into my life, but he let me into his life, and I thank him every day for that. It's a miracle that I can share all my thoughts and worries with him, and he always listens!

BOBBY: We have a great God, and it's wonderful to know that he loves us unconditionally. I could never go back to what I was like before I became a Christian. I've started on a new journey with Jesus, and it brings new and exciting experiences every day. I used to live a very shallow life, but now he has shown me what real love is, and that love has done wonders in my family. He has given us a much deeper love for each other, and I now have a compassion for other people that I simply didn't have before. Jesus loves me so much that I know he will pick me up when I fail him, but I also know that he's helping me not to fall so often. Christianity is a new life, and I praise God for giving it to me.

Well, thank you for taking the time to read our book. We hope and pray that it may have helped you in some way. If you've started on the same road with Jesus that we've been talking about, we hope that somewhere our paths may cross. Always remember that God loves you.

Tommy Cannon and Bobby Ball

And Finally

BOBBY: Just one more joke before we say good-bye.

TOMMY: It's hard being a Christian sometimes!

BOBBY: One day Tommy went to his pastor and confessed that he thought he was guilty of vanity. 'What makes you think that?' asked the pastor. 'Because,' said Tommy, 'every morning when I look in the mirror, I think how handsome I look.' 'Don't worry,' answered the pastor, very reassuringly. 'That isn't a sin, it's a mistake.'

TOMMY: No wonder people call us the only act with two straight men. Say goodbye.

BOBBY: Goodbye, everybody!